THE SECRET WEAPON

I met Sid McNairy when I was in undergrad at Morgan State University. He was my health teacher and an Assistant Coach on the football team, and I was a captain on our basketball team, so I was sure to be attentive in class. The first memory I have of Sid was how he set the standards for health class. Many professors on campus didn't care about attendance as long as you did your work, but in Sid's class we were to be on time or we would not be let in class, and if we missed three days in the semester, we were going to fail. This was not what I was expecting in Intro to Health, and it threw me off until I found out who Sid McNairy really was.

He shared with the class how he woke up every morning at 5:00 a.m. to work out and start his day, and how his discipline was to ensure a successful life for himself, and that he was going to be disciplined and committed to greatness in everything he did.

I believed him, and his message had an impact on me that I didn't fully get at the time. Years later, as our staff was in our fourth year of building the Poly Basketball program, I saw someone on social media speak of Sid Power Yoga in Towson, and I realized it was him. I knew that Sid would be a great yoga guru, but more importantly knew he could bring a perspective to our program that would benefit us all. Now I had to figure out how to get him on board.

After establishing contact, I met with Sid and shared with him our vision for our program. We talked about how he could contribute to our student athletes' development and made a plan to make it happen. Since then, Sid has been our yoga guide, and he provided mentoring, inspirational leadership, and generally a great example of a stand-up man who cares for those around him and loves to push people to be their best.

We are all grateful for what Sid has contributed to our success thus far and can't wait to continue to build with him.

#ourfamilyvsyourteam
#nahiwarrior
#polybasketballfamily

Coach Sam Brand
Poly Technical High School
Men's Basketball
2017, 2018, 2019 3A State Champs

THOSE WHO KNOW GOD

And Those Who Want To Know Him

SID MCNAIRY

Published by: Sid Publishing
1800 The Greens Way, Unit 208
Jacksonville Beach, Fl 32250
www.SidMcNairy.com

Hardback 978-0-9975383-8-0
Paperback 978-0-9975383-6-6
Ebook 978-0-9975383-7-3

Library of Congress Control Number: 2020917788

Cover Photograph by Liz McNairy
Cover Design by Evocative Designs
Interior Design by MediaNeighbours.com
Printed in the United States

Notice
The information in this book is meant to supplement anyone's spiritual practice. The author and publisher advise readers to take full responsibility for their safety and know their limits. Before undertaking a spiritual journey of any sort, please consult your physician if you have been in their care. Before practicing the skills described in this book, be sure you avoid risk beyond your level of experience, aptitude, training and comfort zone.

This book is dedicated to my friends,
Tiffany Avery Smith and Kelly Dunaja,
who showed me that God is everywhere
and that when we accept life as it is, he will
show up through every person we meet.

Tiffany and Kelly, thank you for calling
me forward. I feel you from the other side.
Peace and love always.

CONTENTS

A Warrior's Prayer IX

Foreword by Rob Wergin XII

Preface by Liz McNairy XVII

How It Came to Be XVII

What It Is XX

Acknowledgements XXIII

Introduction XXX

1. Acknowledge you are unaware of the problem 1

2. Determine what is holding you hostage 11
   - Simply know what is there 12
   - You can't clear what you are not aware of ... 12
   - Find Your Voice 13
   - Let's put the past behind us where it belongs, behind us 15

3. Identify how your past is driving your today 17
   - STOP, LISTEN, and FEEL 19
   - All of life is determined by your connection.. 21
   - I choose to clean up after myself 22

4. Establish a new program & transform your life 27
   - So, what is it going to be? 32

5. Clear out the pattern defaults........................ 37
"I'll be damned" 38
Go deeper than your thoughts. It is
all right here for you to awaken to 40

6. Bring new people to the table....................... 47
What is good for the goose
is good for the gander 51
Purge to Surge.. 52
One person's trash is another person's
treasures.. 54

7. Establish a new routine and
put it into action 56
Listen twice as much as you speak 59
The Prayer of Connection............................ 59
All of life is determined by
your connection 64

8. Find those to walk with.................................. 65

9. Let go and live in your highest expression ... 74
Compassion is to have sympathy, genuine
care and concern, for the suffering or
misfortune of others 79
Sin is an immoral act considered
to be transgressive against divine law....... 88
What would your savior do with you? 90

10. Share this with the world.............................. 94

11. Be willing to start again................................ 104
All of life is determined
by your connection 113

A WARRIOR'S PRAYER

(through Sid McNairy)

I call on the Four Directions, as you have established the pillars in my life on the mountain.

To the keepers of the East, the Great Eagle, may you come in and give us and those reading this book the vision to continue to grow and heal in every way, so that all beings on this planet and those who are not on this planet anymore can feel it through this book from your eyes, from your vision that connects us to our highest selves. As you fly the highest of all the beings here, may you lift this book up.

To the keepers of the South, Brother Coyote and Brother Mouse, I ask that you come in and continue to bring the reflections that we see in one another, the reflection of the coyote and the mouse, so people can understand how to let go of sweating the small things and begin to embrace all that is in our way of connecting to our highest selves.

To the keepers of the West, Brother Bear, I ask of you to send your medicine and your healing into this book as you have done in my life, allowing everyone to look within to find their space of healing that helps us all heal in every way.

To the keepers of the North, the Grandmothers, the White Buffalo, the White Buffalo Woman who carried the peace pipe, I ask that you give us the wisdom so that this book will heal hearts and create a deep sense of peace throughout every being that reads *Those Who Know God—And Those Who Want to Know Him*. From this space of peace, let us feel the love that flows from you to all of us.

To all of our relations, to the winged ones, the birds that fly through the sky, to those who swim in the sea, to the creepy crawlers that move on the earth, to the trees, the spirits, and all the others that I may be missing, may you join us as you have joined me on the mountain.

To Mother earth, you have provided us everything in the physical and held us in your arms when we have fallen apart. May you come with us and allow this book to have deep roots, so we can help others reconnect to you so they see their reflection and how they are causing the hurt on the earth—and that when they heal themselves, they will heal you.

And to Creator, the Great Mystery that lies within us all, please come into this book and share your wisdom so that all who read this are open to the possibility that all of life is meant to be joyous and prosperous, and as each person reaches their highest good, all are able to help others do the same.

FOREWORD BY ROB WERGIN

Sid McNairy and I met a few years ago in Flat Rock, North Carolina. He and his newly wed wife, Liz, had registered for a weekend healing immersion I was conducting. Sid was referred by a mutual dear friend and client who in that moment was facing a deadly battle with cancer.

When we first met, there was a recognition, a familiarity, an understanding of the truth of Sid McNairy. A man of deep spiritual beliefs, a man of deep faith, and a man who had "been through it" in this incarnation. Sid also projected deep and powerful energy as a man of healing. He is a man of compassion, and a man of truth. We became friends instantly, and I am deeply honored to write the foreword for his new book, *Those Who Know God*.

You will see into Sid's soul as you read this amazingly powerful yet simple guide to finding God, finding inner peace, and learning to change your life. In changing your life, you will change the lives of all around you as you project the powerful, positive patterns of change.

Are you ready to begin your personal transformation? Are you ready to discover how critical Sid's wisdom is in this time of uncertainty?

The energy in and around the planet is filled with chaos, intensity, uncertainty, worry, fear, anger, and pain. Each week it seems, a book is published writing about corruption, lies, deceit, inappropriate behavior—books creating more chaos, intensity, worry, and fear; books feeding negativity into the collective consciousness. How about a book completely opposite of corruption, chaos, and fear energy? How about a book of truth, humor, and easy to understand principles and techniques? How about a book that will change your life, change your thinking, change your reality?

Sid's book contains hope, humor, humility, and honesty to rise above the best-selling books of darkness. *Those Who Know God* is the perfect antidote for darkness, sadness, and confusion in one's life, and the energy and words within Sid's book create the love and joyful energy so many are now seeking, as we are all hungry and searching for comfort, faith, and direction. Sid's humility, honesty, and clarity return our energies to the energies of love and faith, the energies of possibility and hope, the energies of peace and gratitude, the energies of love coming from inside..., and the energies that satisfy our hunger for comfort, faith, and direction.

How many books have you started, only to be turned away by metaphysical words and exercises sounding too weird or not making sense? How many books have you started, only to be turned away by the book being too religious or too unlike your cultural beliefs?

No one, no religion, no culture is left out of Sid's book of hope and change. We see ceremonies from Native Americans, quotes from Rumi, sports stories, personal stories, references to Christ, Buddha, the Reverend Martin Luther King Jr., William Shakespeare, and lessons from Sid's life experiences.

Many books write of enlightenment, many books write of spiritual and religious goals. The content, the words, and the concepts of many books leave the reader feeling the results are unattainable, there are so many rules and regulations in the path of change or a transformation.

Sid's straightforward approach to life and life's experiences, including our patterns and programs, solicits a curiosity about what is next in his book, and just at the right moment, the curiosity is met by a reflection of his process, leading you to renewed faith in whatever you may have lost your faith in, or leading you to a faith reflecting your energy and your heart's desire, and even more important, leading you to a hunger to finish the book.

Without giving too much away, one of my favorite "Sid techniques" is the "Stop, Listen, and Feel" technique. An amazing and simple way to wake yourself up; identify your old patterns, habits, and programs; and bring your awareness into the moment, instead of always going into the past. Later in his book, he adds the word "clear" to "Stop, Listen, and Feel, and Clear!" to create even more available power to your words and actions as you transform.

Another favorite "Sid technique" is "purge to surge," a technique to propel you into another energy and a deeper understanding of where your life has been, as well as the opportunity to propel your life into the truth you have always wished for.

There are too many gems in Sid's book to mention in detail. However, I would like to mention another. There is a powerful forgiveness exercise, "The Prayer of Connection," written by Sid, that is a call to walk and share your newly learned power from this book with others as you walk your new talk and walk the planet.

Applying the techniques from my dear friend Sid's book will create changes within you and create changes within your life. Also, critical in the world today, you will assist in the vital change in your energy and the energy you project into the collective consciousness, at a time when all our futures are at stake.

Rob Wergin
Conduit of Divine Energy
From the Documentary *Heal*

PREFACE BY LIZ MCNAIRY

How It Came to Be

Twenty-one days. I witnessed Sid put pen to paper to write this book in just 21 days. Since I have known Sid, I have known one of his greatest gifts to be his determination. So, when he set out to complete this in 30 days and finished in 21, it was no surprise to me. His determination is felt throughout *Those Who Know God* in his direct delivery, his recommendation to read this book as fast as you can, and to complete the exercises as fully as possible.

The inspiration for the book began back in 2016. At that time, I saw people who were coming to Sid, asking him for help to heal all sorts of ailments: mental, physical, emotional, and spiritual. I witnessed that healing would take place for these people, sometimes in a matter of moments, sometimes longer. Each time I felt like I was witnessing a miracle.

However, what would also show up was physical pain in Sid's body. The pain would present itself through inflammation, atrophy of muscles, physical sensitivity, and more. At the time, we did not know what was happening. We thought it was a reaction to food.

It was the end of 2016, right around Christmas time, that Sid was in such pain that he could not even get out of bed for ten days.

We began to learn that this pain was coming from the healing that was occurring in those he worked with.

This was the beginning of Sid's quest to heal himself in order to be able to stand for others in their own healing. He had to figure out a way to continue to help people without taking on their pains, in turn creating more pain in the world.

During that time, Sid went through lessons of evolution that led to us leaving our house and creating the steps that birthed this book.

As part of those steps, we hired a business coach to help us find our way to make being on the road sustainable. Our coach told us that some people she was working with were just going through the process to bring forward their next expression in the world. Here we were, thinking we had all the programs we needed, only to find that our journey had just begun.

We traveled 31,000 miles in our car in one year. Each and every one of those days found us living the experiences described in the eleven chapters that follow. One of the foundational teachings—"Stop. Listen. Feel"—was the guiding light for me.

Prior to the start of this journey, I was halfway through my requirements to obtain my license for counseling in the state of Maryland. As I moved through the routine of day to day, I was on autopilot. I was moving through the checklist of what I thought I should be doing. All the while, there was an internal knowing that this was not the path for me. I was becoming more stressed every day. I was running all over town to provide services. Most importantly to me, I was allowing myself to be shaped by viewpoints and teachings that I did not align with. In psychology this is referred to as *cognitive dissonance*: the state of acting in a way that goes against your belief. This experience was present for me in the life I was living, and I knew it was time to move on.

As we hit the road that May, we allowed STOP, LISTEN, FEEL to guide us in each step of the way.

We asked for guidance from something bigger than ourselves, and we had faith through every step that the path was destined for us.

It was amazing to see as Sid began to release the pains and release them for good. The real test came when he would be called to work with someone. I was always extra prayerful during these times, to keep Sid and all those around him healthy.

I started to see a divine orchestration of our life taking place. It was as if we were flexing a muscle called "faith," and each time we worked it, the muscle of faith grew stronger and stronger.

What It Is

Those Who Know God is a guidebook to help increase the space of connection to something bigger for you and your life. In each chapter you will have the opportunity to take a lesson away with you that you can immediately begin to implement in your life.

Often we have a tendency to think that we know what the problem in our life is. The first chapter is designed to offer the reader the possibility that they actually do *not* know. It describes what it is to slow down and pause. When we slow down and step out of "autopilot," we have the chance to go deeper and begin to create a fresh start.

With the next chapter, the reader is asked to dive deeper to discover a profound level of the problem. This comes after taking the time to consider that you do not know the answer. From a blank slate, a new possibility begins to take shape. Way down, in the whispers of the heart, lies the answer.

In chapter three, the reader becomes responsible for understanding their past, the old

Program, and how it is continuing to show up in the present day. With this step, it is important to take the time to be with the old program. To see it and feel it, is to understand it.

Next is to begin to establish a new way. Once the past is cleared, you can begin to center yourself into what you desire and build a new program through conscious choice.

Chapter five is dedicated to seeing the old patterns show up, and then consciously choosing a new place to go.

The next step and chapter begins to describe the power of letting go. It includes information on "Purge to Surge," the process of dedicating 30 days to letting go of physical, tangible items, which gives way to a bigger, internal process of letting go.

In chapter seven, you will read about establishing a new routine to support you in the direction you desire to go. Along with the steps to bring forward your new routine, Sid shares his own "The Prayer of Connection" to aid in the process of forgiveness and compassion.

With chapter eight, Sid shares the importance of coaches and accountability buddies—people in your life that help you stay aligned with your highest. You will be given the opportunity to evaluate your tribe of people surrounding you and reflect on just how they are impacting you.

As you begin to near the end of the book, chapter nine calls for you to live in the consciousness of your chosen way. With a powerful forgiveness exercise, this chapter helps you to continue to be in the practice of moving forward with compassion for yourself and those in your life.

Chapter ten is dedicated to inspiring the reader to share their process with the world. At times this may be through words, and yet there is great power in simply being the example for others to see.

The final chapter, eleven, reminds the reader that there is always the space to begin again. As we all continue to evolve, this can, at times, look like coming back to step one. This is different from going "back." We can never truly go back. Each time we revisit the book, it is with a new perspective, because we have already been through the process, and our programs have shifted.

Keep going until all is clear and live in the practice.

Liz McNairy
Wife of Sid McNairy
Life Empowerment Coach

ACKNOWLEDGEMENTS

As I sit at the end or beginning of this amazing journey of writing *Those Who Know God,* I am taking a moment to acknowledge all the love that helped bring forward this book that will impact lives for many years to come.

God, I am grateful for all that you have created in my life. You have shown me that, with you behind me, everything is possible. I give thanks for all of the sages, spiritual teachers, mystics, rule clearers, and more that have paved the way for us all to continue to bring light and love into the world. I am grateful for our time as I pause and pray. I sit to meditate, and I see an eagle or hawk. I go to surf, and the dolphins come. I wake up to say good morning to my wife, I hear from a friend, I break bread with a stranger, and all the other moments I am reminded you are here with me as I take this journey. Thank you, and I love you more than words can say.

To the dear one, Tiffany Avery Smith, thank you for calling me forward. I often think back to many moments that led me further on my path. Texting back and forth only to fly out and spend three days sharing all I knew at the time. Seeing the signs as the preacher came, and we heard him repeat what we had come to be in our conversations. "Again, truly I tell you that if two of you on earth agree about anything they ask for, it will be done for them by my Father in heaven." (Matthew 18:19) I give thanks for the many gifts from that day forward, sharing meditations, introduction to Rob, time with you, Rick, and the kids, being an angel in disguise at our wedding, and so much more. I am grateful for the thousands who came together because of you. Thank you for keeping us straight from "The Other Side." Love you, always.

Kelly Dunaja, another one who helped me come forward into me, as fully as I could imagine at the time. Thank you for believing in me and picking up the phone. We gained four more years than they said, and I am grateful you taught me so much about me. I know I will see you again as time will pass. You are my soul sister, for sure.

I also am grateful for my wife, best friend, lover, supporter, and teacher, Liz McNairy. You have taught me so many things—most importantly, how to love myself and to love another more fully in every way. Thank you for being so amazing as you have helped me stay the course to bring this book forward. Thank you for being my travel buddy as we have moved around the world and touched the lives of those we have met and those we did not even know were watching us. I am grateful to continue to move forward with love, with you, as we continue to do God's work together.

To my blood family, Mom, Dad, Sister, Brother, my kids, grandmothers, grandfathers, aunts, uncles, nieces, many many many cousins, and all the future ones. I am grateful for each of you as you touch my life daily and have shown me time and time again how we are leaving our mark through family with every breath that we take. Thank you for continuing to step forward, as I know our way of family is touching lives no matter what arena we step into.

To my brother-in-law, Steve Wilson, I want to make sure you know I am grateful for the love you show with my nieces and my sister. To know that my sister is cared for like the queen she is, there are no words to describe the depth of gratitude in my heart. Thank you for your service to our country and for being someone I know I can call on any time. Please know that you can do the same.

When thinking of who to ask to write the foreword for my book *Those Who Know God*, I knew I had one thought in mind: someone who knows me and that I love. That person is Rob Wergin. I will always remember the chain of moments that brought us together and have kept us in each other's life. I am forever grateful for how all things line up for everyone's highest to come through. Your way of being in the world is an inspiration that I am grateful to get to witness and grow from. Thank you for being a compassionate healer of souls and sharing the divine energy in the world the way you do. I remember when you had your hands on my shoulders and said, "When we come together, the world will heal fast." Well it has begun, and I am grateful to walk with you as my brother.

To Grandmother Morningstar, I am grateful for you continuing to show up at the perfect time. Thank you for being such a guiding light in the world. I know this is another step to completing the mission and healing the land. Thank you for being who you are.

To Maureen Hahn, I am grateful for you and getting to see the love you are. I know you come by it honestly from your mom to all the children you have passed it to. I see it in your daughter, I see it every time you get me some sweet tea. Thank you for all we have come to. Know I love you, as we both do.

To Amanda Shields, I am grateful first for your commitment to our friendship and the way you continue to stand for us in that way. I am grateful to have had the pleasure to move on this journey with you and the many like you. Just acknowledging the truth of the beauty of who you are.

To my brand consultant, Nikki Terry of Orange Custard Design Studio, thank you for helping me find my way through so many possibilities along the way. Thank you for being such a powerful woman to help me find my whole voice to bring forward in such a grand way.

Thank you to my image consultant, Kerry Brett, the host of *The Shot at Love* podcast and photographer. Your words came at the right time, as usual, to help me move forward in so many ways—thank you.

To Ashla Faulkner, for your countless hours as we reached for a book cover worthy of the guts of this book, and thank you, Evocative Designs, for completing the book cover and allowing the impact of this book to be seen as it lays down the first impression in a grand way.

Laurel Ley, you might say that you are a major reason why we came to Jacksonville. Thank you for your listening to spirit when prompted to read the book, and then offering to edit this book. I am grateful for your effort in making sure all points of this book said all I wanted and needed to say to make sure all would receive what is available, moving forward. Thank you for the deep dive of looking through every gem to find the gold at the end.

I am grateful to Ken Rochon (*WhyInfluence.life*). The moment we began to work on my first book and now as we continue the process with

Those Who Know God, we have been linked for the common good of expansion into the next realm. I am also grateful for the introduction to Evelyn Gwynn of Samech Freelance Writing. I am grateful for you, Evelyn, as your care, deep introspection, and guidance will continue to make sure that *Those Who Know God* will continue to spread to the farthest reach around the globe. Thank you for your care and work as we continue to move this far beyond our wildest dreams.

Mary Neighbour, thank you for being there as I finished each book. Thank you for the love you put into your work as we continue to bring these books forward for everyone to digest and move forward in a grand way. Here is to the many more to come.

To my world family, every single human I have met and yet to meet: You inspire me daily to lift up and keep going. You inspire me as I know we all have borrowed this earth from the future ones to come. I am grateful for every kind act you do for a stranger and for those you know. I am grateful for the times as you forgive one another and help all find a new way. I am grateful for the love and compassion you share, as we are all better for it. I am grateful for you picking up *Those Who Know God* and allowing it to set in. Thank you, thank you, thank you. We are the ones that will lift up our world in every way.

Enjoy the journey. I am blessed and full of gratitude for all who have picked up this book, as all of our work will continue to bring the world into a better place for all. May you enjoy all the pages to come.

INTRODUCTION

This book is here for you, no matter where you are on your journey. As I sat down to write, I had you in mind. What could I share that would allow you to connect and lift up your life to your greatest potential, in every way possible? I wanted to share with you some of the lessons of my life that have allowed me to move forward into my best life ever.

In sharing with you the experiences of my lifetime, it is nothing short of amazing to see the impact on those who have read *Those Who Know God*. My 40-plus years of meditation have guided me through a process that has allowed me to move beyond the past and into a new present.

You have picked up this book for a reason, and now you can move forward. This is an opportunity to create the life of your dreams. This is the time for you, and I am excited for you.

Watch your hesitations, as they will become your actions. The actions you take over time create the perception of your character, and our character attracts your reality, over time.

Let me say that again: Watch your hesitations, as they will become your actions. The actions you take over time create the perception of your character, and our character attracts your reality, over time.

As you pick this up, I suggest you read it as fast as you can. Then go back, read it again, and allow it to sink in. Then stay in the process offered in the book until you are moving in the direction you want. We are all creating our reality, whether we know it or not. No matter who you are, one thing for sure is that we all dream. You and I both are living a dream right now. It is up to us, based on our experiences, to set the tone of how our dream will unfold.

So, let's get into it and see just what is possible for you. There is so much to say about this book, and I want you to get going. There is no reason to delay when what you are here for is to connect to love and live it in every way.

The time is now. Read further, and let's get closer together. Remember that this is a book of stories and lessons to help you move forward to live the life of your dreams. There is no need to make this the only way. The truth is the truth, and it is often delivered in different ways. You may have heard some of these concepts before, just put them into action and move forward.

Get into the instinct of flow. This book is about knowing how to find clearing and connection, also known as the flow of life, and live from it all the time. You have an opportunity to reach your highest expression in every way—like the people who achieved the greatest of all times in their fields knew.

Why are great athletes loved? Why are doctors appreciated? Why are entertainers adored? Why are the moms and dads for many loved and cherished? Because all of these people are in the flow of life, and they find a level of presence and connection that keeps them moving forward. Presence and connection lead us to enlightenment.

Enlightenment is about knowing how to turn the light on full blast, in each and every step of life. You are enlightened, now let's turn the light up a bit. Enjoy the ride and see what being enlightened can create for you.

Over the years I have had an opportunity to witness many miracles. I have seen people transform their cancer, HIV, stand up and get out of wheelchairs, and more. What I know is no matter what you are looking for, it is all possible. Let it come in for you.

If you did not know it before, know that you are the key. Like a piece of coal becomes a diamond when the exact amount of pressure is applied, you are becoming your greatest expression. You are being birthed into a diamond every day. Let go and trust the process. It is all there for you.

Here is how it all works: When you understand that all is within you, the fullness of the journey begins.

What I have found is the quest for enlightenment within is a process, as the Buddha found. I have also found that reaching for the perfection of Christ's love has challenged me, over and over again, to be my version of a better man. The space has been building, and like you, I have been seeking what has been dormant inside of me in every way. All we are looking for resides in the depth of your soul. As the old saying goes:

What You Seek Is Seeking You
~ Rumi

Boy, did I spend a lot of time seeking. For many years I looked to see what would elevate the space in me to achieve happiness in a way that would set me free from the patterns of my life. I was caught in a cycle that had me "running on the hamster wheel of life." I believed early on that I could do anything and achieve whatever I wanted. I was guided to the life path those around me had been on. I began to feel that if I didn't get the right grades, I wouldn't get accepted to the right college. If I didn't get into the right college, I wouldn't get the right job.

Without the right job, how would I afford the best car, house, and all of life's finest? I feared that without all the stuff, I wouldn't want to be in my life, nor would the woman of my dreams.

As I looked back, I came to realize the cycle in my mind continued to recreate the pains of my past. This included my days in school at Purdue University, to my 12 years of coaching college football, to my life as a yogi. By this point, I rebuilt my life three times, through two marriages and a long relationship. I look back and remember searching for a woman to complete me. I thought to myself: *I will have to be "this way" in order to be loved.*

When I began to contemplate my life, many of my friends were also football coaches. There were so many in that town, in that place and lifestyle. Somehow, they seemed happy in their marriages and in the game, while I wasn't. I was in a struggle; so I moved into another phase. To try to find happiness, I went from coaching football, to owning yoga studios, teaching yoga, and training teachers. I reinvented myself to fit the picture in my head. I would go on and shift again and again, to bestselling author, musician, artist, healer. You name it, I wanted to find what I thought would complete me.

Throughout that time, I came in and out of fear and had glimpses of happiness. I would come in and out of many emotions. What came to my understanding was that even if I was 99 percent happy, at peace, and/or in love, the 1 percent I felt was missing meant I did not truly have happiness, peace, or love within. It was up to me to live it all at 100 percent, and it was going to be an inside job.

In looking back, the big moment of spiritual bankruptcy came when I was coaching football. I got a glimpse of peace within that came into my being and sent me on a spiral. I began to move down a rabbit hole that would keep going until it was complete. The awakenings started as pain in my body, igniting physical and emotional feelings that would drive me back inside. Surgeries that were done on my ankle caused a shift in my foundation that went from my physical body to my emotions, and eventually shifted my life in every way.

I became a new person in my internal operating system. From a new foundation, I began to transform. Over time, I learned to shift my parenting, and my relationships transformed in every aspect. It showed up so strongly in my connection to me that as I cleared my programs, I even lost 75 pounds, as my wife and I went on a year-long tour of the earth. We drove 31,000 miles, plus international flights, all in a year.

I became a new person as I cleared. As my evolution unfolded, every person I came in contact with helped me to see me. As I was continually becoming new from each interaction, everywhere I showed up was new. Everywhere I became new because I was new.

My foundation was revealing itself and creating a new place to help others in life, no matter where they were coming from. At one point, we went over the birth dates and zodiac signs of everyone in our advance training. We were looking at numerology. Then it dawned on me that everyone was an aspect of me. One person had my son's zodiac sign, another had my other son's sign, my daughter's sign, my brother and sister who are the same sign, and then my mother and father. I was able to see how I was evolving everywhere I was.

The connection to my greatest teacher within was found in my understanding of how we are all connected as one. This showed in everyone I came in contact with. It was a deeper awakening than I was anticipating when I was sitting in the chair of the teacher. I have had a remarkable transformation. Through this book, now is your chance to take the ride.

What I can say of the teacher-student relationship is this: When the teacher is ready, the students will come, because the teacher is ready to evolve. Be sure you read that for what it said. Watch how your mind creates from the Program it is running. Reading the line "when the teacher is ready, the students will come," you easily can perceive what is familiar versus what is really being said.

We often learn by teaching, because as the old concept goes, *we teach most what we need to learn*. I have seen that I have had to be willing to see myself in a way that allows me to shift within myself. I could see how greatness was being birthed everywhere I went, through my interactions with so many.

I have had the pleasure of seeing so many great shifts in the world through others. As I introduce this book, I want to share with you "Sally," who made major shifts as we worked together through life. Let me say thanks to Sally for allowing me to share her story in this way.

Even though Sally grew up with a silver spoon in her mouth, despite having everything she could think of, she felt alone and broken. Most people could not see the internal suffering that was taking place. Sally had been a high-level executive for an advertising company, had a great husband, and three kids she adored. Yet a typical day since leaving the firm found her longing for a chance to breathe.

An ordinary day for Sally looked like waking up and getting the kids ready for school. While the kids were eating, Sally would finish getting ready. Saddened by what she saw in the mirror, she would start the day criticizing herself and begin to experience headaches and back pain. After a full day, Sally would close the night self-medicating on the porch, looking at the stars, before getting a few hours of sleep and then starting again. Self-medicating alone on the porch would come to be known as "taking out the trash."

One day Sally found her way to our wellness center. She walked in with her hat pulled down over her eyes, as she avoided making eye contact with strangers. What she noticed was that it was different than all of the other studios and centers she had been to before. After her first class, she got into her Range Rover only to find herself crying and crying, as if the tears would never stop. Something strange happened, and she noticed she felt better. It was a clearing from her emotional body that would allow the light to flow in, and something seemed more clear. What Sally knew was that she wanted more of that.

A week would go by before she came back to the center. When her typical anxiety crept in, she remembered the unfamiliar sense of peace she had experienced after taking classes, and she began to feel a bit lighter. She was beginning to connect to a new place of being. One day she came into the center, her hat a little higher and her eyes began to peak through.

This is when we met and a connection was made. The connection would cause a chain reaction that would forever change the trajectory of

Sally's life. I recall many moments of Sally coming in as her meditative quality grew more and more evident. As time would pass, her friends would point out that there was something different about her. She had a glow that was beginning to show in her day-to-day walk.

Sally took on programs such as "Yoga and Life Empowerment" as if she knew what was at stake. It was not only her happiness, it was also her kids' happiness, her connection with her husband, her connection with her parents, and her connection with her community. As she continued to practice yoga over the next couple of years, feeling better became her mission.

One day Sally was asked if she ever thought about becoming a person to empower others' lives. Her response was, "No, how could I, I am finding my own power. I never thought of me doing this." She was offered an application and took it with her. When she got out to the car, she put it on the passenger seat. On this particular Saturday morning, she had driven her husband's car.

Days would pass, and she would find herself at lunch, getting coffee, in the carpool lane, and friends began to lean on her just to share their moments of pain and anxiety. Little did she know that everyone around her was being impacted from her new-found connection inside. As she was evolving, her world was shifting for the better.

One night when her husband came home, he walked in and said, "Hey, did you leave this application in my car?"

Sally replied, "Application? I'm not sure."

"Here it is. It seems to be from the center you have been going to," her husband responded.

"Oh yeah, they thought I would be good at empowering others," Sally said.

Her husband paused and then replied, "Well, here it is. Are you going to do it? I think you should. You are happy there, and it may just be the thing--"

"The thing? What do you mean?" Sally said, with a little edge to her voice.

"The thing you have been looking for, the belief in something more, the chance to have meaning to your life, the belief that the world will be a better place, and you can be the difference," her husband responded.

Months would go by and Sally would look at the questions and sometimes cry. Something was happening. Sally was gaining confidence. The day before the training, Sally turned in her application to begin Phase I. From day one, Sally was all in. She began opening up and, as we say, she "cleared up her side of the street." It was amazing to watch the unfolding.

Sally was shining with more confidence every day. What I knew was this was all possible for everyone who takes the time to connect to the highest power inside.

What I have seen is often people need to slow down, get still, and let the garbage come to the surface and pass by. This is "STOP, LISTEN, and FEEL," or as we call it, SLF, for short. I am blessed to have worked with thousands of people who transformed their connection to hurt, guilt, shame, sadness, fear, and more into optimism, joy, happiness, peace, and love. They found that their lives have shifted beyond their wildest dreams.

Sally had been through a lot, much of which we all can relate to. Some of Sally's past has been beyond what anyone should experience. What we can all relate to are the feelings that come along with another's experience. The moments many come through are the pain points where we can get stuck along the way. If we allow ourselves to keep going and:

STOP: completely learn to be still so our minds can be seen.

LISTEN: to ourselves so we can hear from the connection deep within.

FEEL: so we can know where we can head next, in order to reach our highest connection and possibility.

There is only so much one can face in the world, and what may seem small to one is large to another and *vice versa*. Those who are harmed as children are often the ones to share the most light with the world. As we move forward in this book, I am excited for all who will open up to get to the other side and live your dream life.

There are truths around us that will set us free if we are open to allowing them to sink in fully. Seeing the truth will set you free. The truth I have uncovered while working with so many people over the years is:

All of life is determined by your connection!

Read it again:

All of life is determined by your connection!

Now, let's take a moment to look at what's next. As you enter this journey, moving from the dark to the light, know there is greatness in both. Be open to allowing it all to be good. All of it is helping you see the good in everything.

As you read this book, know there will be times to reflect and go deeper. Take a moment to pause—walk away if needed, and reflect. This book will help you STOP, LISTEN, and FEEL.

It is your time to be willing to feel in order to heal in every way of your life. This is your time to enjoy it. I look forward to hearing of your transformations to come.

1 ACKNOWLEDGE YOU ARE UNAWARE OF THE PROBLEM.

There is a space that we all reside in. We are either clear or we are not. To be clear is to allow your mind to arrive and stay centered on the present moment. In this state of being clear, you are able to maintain a sense of connection to what is at hand. By remaining clear we are able to bring forward all of life's possibilities. It is truly an understanding that from a place of clarity we can open up to a clear connection that will allow all to come forward.

As I had seen for myself, I am 100 percent of something, or I am not that something. If I am in a place that is 99 percent of something and 1 percent not, then I am not 100 percent of that which I wish to be.

I desire peace. If I am at 95 percent peace and 5 percent angry, I am not in the state of peace. The 5 percent anger occupies the space I live in. This is where the work is. Get clear and move into 100 percent of what you desire, beyond the Program. The Program is what is running in the background.

As you begin to clear, you will hear the inner voice in the background that is guiding your life forward. Within the overall operating system, everyone has many echo-programs that continue to evolve over time. Keep going and clear all Programs that are not serving your highest good.

Become aware of the Program that is running your life until you awaken to the clarity to move forward. It is there—keep going until the clarity is with you. It is the old outdated Program that is managing the experience and just when you think you have cleared it, it rears its head. It is the old, outdated Program, the "go to" director that takes over when you are onto something more. Continue to move forward, that is what we are doing. Clearing the old and consciously moving to the life of your dreams.

Have you ever been on a mission, big or small, and all of a sudden that mission seems to be sabotaged? You could be going for your dream job, and you may have even made it through your first interview, only to feel something fall short. You may have been so happy about the first interview that you tell your best friend, and he or she says to you, "Well, you know they are interviewing other people."

Guess what? That is all a mirror reflecting from the voice of the outdated Program running inside of you.

It's like the snake in the bushes. Most days you won't see it; yet when it needs to back you up, it will be seen.

Now is the time to pull the snakes out of you and send them on their way. Begin to take notice. Notice the patterns that are revealed. STOP: observe yourself as you move. LISTEN: see yourself as you allow your thoughts to come in. FEEL: sit with what is present, remain unattached as it passes through. SLF: This is where you begin your shifts to evolve to your new programs. Sit with all that comes up. Be willing to FEEL until you have cleared and are ready to move forward. No need to run—if it gets overwhelming, advance with a balanced mind and allow all to pass in its time.

Imagine the Program is a weed. If you start to dig the weed up and rush, you will likely break the roots into several parts. In this case, you will come back and have more weeds to tend to in time. By advancing slowly, you have lifted the weed closer to the surface. Now, from a place of being centered, you can come back and clear the root of the Program.

Let's look at the truth, as this level of truth is where you will be set free. The truth we are speaking of is "what is true or in accordance to fact or reality." (All definitions are from *Oxford*

Languages.) There is also your truth that, going forward, we will refer to as your "perspective." Your truth or perspective can be shifted at any point in time that you desire to make the shift, using the tools of SLF. The greater truth will stand through the test of time. This is where you get to clear out the snakes and uncover the jewels. Know that this is not good or bad, right or wrong; this has been your way of experiencing life. It is strictly the Program that is holding you back from being 100 percent clear to move forward into the life of your dreams.

All of your actions today are driven from the past. It's time to clear and be open to being something new in this moment. Be willing to establish discipline in your life and in yourself. It is the discipline to go for your dreams that will set you free. If you are reaching for peace, you must become a disciple to peace. As the discipleship opens, you will grow into a state of leadership to move on and know you must first be willing to be in the discipleship of what it is you want to bring forward.

If you continue to see the Program (your current way of being) as a sense of power, as a place of comfort, you will continue to hold onto it. Now is your time to move forward. The life of your dreams is yours to have.

You picked up this book. Truth. You are looking for something more. Let it in.

No matter . . . what, there is something.

No matter . . . how small, let's get it.

We can eradicate the darkness and bring in the light.

Only the light can remove the darkness.
~ Dr. Martin Luther King Jr.

STOP: take the time to look in the mirror. Without the mirror, you cannot see your own face.

Let that sink in: you can't see your own face. You can't see the root of your Program. You have to allow yourself to look in the mirror. Get still and know. Your mind is moving and drawing it all to you.

LISTEN: to those you have invited in your life from a place of love; listen to those who love you. Listen deep within. It is there that all can be revealed. Drop your defenses that are coming from the old Program that has been running you. Be willing to be vulnerable and listen. Remember it is not good or bad, right or wrong, it just is. It is just where you are moving from. So, let's go and see where you can move from going forward.

FEEL: Open up and allow it all to come through. Get clear, see what is embedded within. You are safe here. The kid who was wounded is here and can trust in the person you are now to handle anything needed to move on. No one can hurt you. The feeling is within you;

you can put it down and release it. Let's look at it clearly. You are in a place, sitting in a chair or standing somewhere. Where exactly are you? Recognize the truth of it. Are you living in your mind or is this taking place right where you are? That is what happened in the past; it is not likely the situation where you are now. If this is happening now and there is a threat, find help and remove this immediate threat.

Before we move on, I want to differentiate between physical, emotional, mental, and spiritual threats. If there is an immediate physical threat in front of you, get help NOW. Put down this book and find someone who can help you move forward from this place of harm.

As we look at the emotional, mental, and spiritual threats, it is important to understand threats are made bigger in the power of your perception—your perception as it relates to your truth and not the truth. One point of this book is to get you to FEEL. To get you to be real with yourself and to connect the Program and its power to hold you where you are. Know you have the ability to move beyond. The point of this book is to get you free, so you can live the absolute best life that is meant for you.

Until you are aware of the Program you won't move on. It's about getting you to zero. Getting you to a point of nothing at all. Nothing, a zero point that allows what is new to be birthed. Look at it. If you are carrying 5, 4, 3, 2, or 1 percent of the old Program, you are unable to reach 100 percent of the fullness of what you desire.

-1,000	-100	-10	(0)	+10	+100	+1,000
	Negative		Zero		Positive	

That's it, zero or nothing is the point where all else grows from. Look at life as zero or nothing being the middle; if you fall into the past you have fallen back into the negative. You continue to drop back to what was: the problems, the experience of hurt, guilt, shame. Zero or nothing allows you the space so you can move on into what can come forward. At zero you gain access to love, peace, unity, optimism, and more.

Continue to find zero or nothing so you can move forward. Should you slip to the negative, pause and come back. Get free of the past. Let go and get back to zero or nothing, and allow yourself to move forward into your new present.

I had the pleasure of working with a couple who wanted to clear up their relationship. The problem *now* wasn't what had taken place. That was the past, and it wasn't going to change. The problem was in allowing themselves to move forward. They each had their own Program that was running their relationship, that would pull them back into the hurt, despair, anger, and into the junk that kept them in this state.

Let's examine the dynamic of relationships on an intimate level. Most people come into a relationship with new expectations. It can go something like this: Before getting in the relationship, one person, if not both, had been in other relationships and maybe had intimate relationships before meeting. Somehow, despite all of what had taken place before, both parties choose to go into the relationship and shift into new dynamics. Sounds great thus far.

As soon as something disrupts that new dynamic, often there is a breakdown because one or both parties fall back into an old Program. Not right or wrong, not good or bad, just is. Know that it is okay for you to have feelings around this; yet it truly is just what it is. A way to stay clear of this is to STOP and allow your mind to pause. LISTEN to the voice in the background, and FEEL what you are experiencing in the moment. Get to zero, or nothing before it ever becomes part of a new pattern.

It was a challenge for the wife to move beyond seeing her husband as anything different than what took place. She could see how he was a great father. That he was great at his job. Even that he was a great husband. Then her Program would kick in. You could see it coming in. Her body language would shrink back, her jaw would clench, her hands would begin to move. She couldn't see what was happening.

Her reaction wasn't only predicated on what had happened with her husband, it included what was in her life before her husband ever came around; i.e., her program. You see, he was acceptable when he was the life of the party. He was fine when he drank with the staff, maybe even flirted a bit. Yet when the Program kicked in, all bets were off. A new dynamic started with his actions; and there, t\he Program began to run on overdrive. When his actions changed beyond the expected, her operating system of fear took over. Yes, he had to clear up his stuff, and if she was willing to go deeper, from zero or nothing, they could move forward.

Once they got clear, it was awesome to watch. They would sit close and pat each other on the knee. Their relationship was moving forward in so many ways. When their Programs would take over, they would become more distant physically and emotionally.

Once at zero or nothing, they would have to have the discipline to go on. They would have to hold their own discipleship to their marriage and each other, to stay focused on the relationship of their desires. To be in discipleship is to make a commitment to yourself to see it through to get to 100 percent of your desire. That is the work for all of us, to come into discipleship with what we want, whether it is relationship, health, with spirit, or anything else. In a partnership of any sort, we will have to come into discipleship to hold up our end of the relationship.

Often we just need to pause to get the full picture and move on to the next step

Reflection

What are your takeaways from this chapter? Let's apply the practice of STOP, LISTEN, and FEEL. Look for how the Program is running in your life, and what it is bringing that you don't want.

STOP: Pause, breathe, let yourself be open to what is here now.

LISTEN: Take some time and hear what your mind is saying. Remember there is nothing right or wrong, good or bad. Just begin to hear and see how things are showing up for you. How do you view life now? Is this different from how you want to live your life?

FEEL: Start to understand your feelings. No reactions, move forward to what you desire. What is it that is guiding you, and in what direction are you choosing to go?

2 DETERMINE WHAT IS HOLDING YOU HOSTAGE.

I love movies. I have seen a great deal of movies about being possessed. It is interesting to observe the commonality of how to get demons to leave. I have even talked to priests who do work to help release a demon from the host body. The common space to get rid of the demon is to get it to say its name. Once the name is revealed, it is then ready to leave.

Similar to this, you are playing host to something you no longer wish to have around. Start by seeing if you can identify the Program that is running you. Let the name come forward. Can you identify what is holding you hostage to the past? See if you can identify it. Simply know what it is as you identify it. Release the need to make it you. Release the need to allow it to define you.

Simply know what is there.

Check in to see just what is coming through. By beginning to give it a name, you have a chance to see when it surfaces and create space to allow it to pass on. Where in your body is it? There is some association you have with it, and it will speak to you at some point. STOP, LISTEN, FEEL. There is a cellular memory that comes with our experiences when we attach to a memory of a moment, and it lands within our body. The storage of our brain comes in at a cellular level. Where is it in your body?

Listen to your heart. What does it say before your mind takes over and begins to filter all that is coming forward? Your heart whispers from the universal truth. Your mind screams from the fear of survival based on your past.

You can't clear what you are not aware of.

Go deeper, there is hope. God can see it all. Connect there; ask for help. You can let go, and let it be. Imagine you want to clear your beautiful, white marble floors. It is easy to see the major dirt. If you spill coffee grounds on the floor, you would see them clearly. You would sweep, then dust, then mop, and *voila*, you have clean floors.

Now imagine your life as a white marble floor, and someone spilled powdered sugar on it. You may not know it is there, until one day, it may get a little sticky. Then, after getting a different perspective, you can see what is there and you can clean it up. Let's get down, maybe on our knees, ask for help, and clean it up. Clean up your side of the street. We will discuss this more in depth later.

Let's look at your Program from your past experiences. How old were you when you first felt it? Remember: STOP and LISTEN to your heart. FEEL what is there. Just be willing to experience deep enough for it to surface.

Your body is your temple. It houses your soul essence. Just where can you look in and move forward?

Where was the moment taking place? Was this in your childhood, was it in teen years, more recent, or was this long before? LISTEN. You may want to journal this, and let it all go.

Who was there with you? What part were they playing in the moment? Look deep in; it is stored in the memory of your cells. Let it be uncovered.

Find Your Voice.

Within us is a vibration. Connect to the vibration and find the place within that shifts as the frequency shifts. Go in: STOP, LISTEN, FEEL.

What was it you wanted to say? As we look back, we may realize we did not have the words to speak to what was. Find the words now. We may have been scared to share. Find the words now. This is part of your work to get clear and know.

What was it you wanted to say? As the past clears, you will find the words that complete the shift. What was it the people who were involved in the moment wanted to say to you? Often when we are remembering a moment, we are left interpreting what is being said. Go in and see what the true message is.

For many years, I held onto parts of my childhood that I felt were not good enough. No matter how much peace I came into, I was stuck. What I did not know was I was stuck in the memory of my DNA.

My spankings were really a deep uncovering of the trauma of my Native American and African ancestral trauma for years. I did not know it was there, let alone how to put the rage into words. I took many years to see how this was stuck within. It was stuck on so many layers -1, -10, -100, -1000, who knew? It was deep. Once I put a name to it—slavery, relocation, genocide—I then could move forward. There are deep layers within, which many of us have no words for, because it was there long before we came into this life. You are here now. STOP, let it come, be gentle with yourself. LISTEN, ask what your body is telling you, amid the whispers of your heart. FEEL, and let it go.

I see how the connection or lack of connection to the greater truth causes it to be harder to get out of the pains of the past. This is why it is important to get real, here and now, so we can all move forward. We need our voice deep within to be heard. Keep doing the work. If you find yourself stuck in the pain, go beyond, and keep doing the work. Move yourself to zero or nothing. Now is the time we will transform this together and move forward.

Let's put the past behind us where it belongs, behind us.

I see the world and where many have gotten stuck. Stuck in the past of what we have been told or experienced. For me, I was not told directly many of the things that became my Programs. Often I created an echo-program based on many of the things I was hearing and experiencing in my life. I recall watching *Roots*, the movie and series.

I remember watching *Back to the Future*. I had a creative mind then, as I do now. Because I could imagine I could go back in time, the Program shifted from being scared to deep rage and wanting to wipe out those enslaving others. It was already there in my DNA; yet the combination of my experience and what I was told allowed the rage to be activated. It is something I know is there, and today I choose to see it and move away from it.

Each is part of the whole. Just as strong as the light in someone is the amount of darkness. I make a conscious choice of where I will live from. We can all choose love and light. By making this choice, we are choosing to live from zero and forward. Eventually what we all can capture is that the dark space is so distant, we no longer need to play in that connection. It is a product of our experiences, even the ones we are not aware of. STOP, see just what is shaping your state of mind. LISTEN, to how your thoughts are playing into what is happening in your everyday life. FEEL, and move beyond it.

3 IDENTIFY HOW YOUR PAST IS DRIVING YOUR TODAY.

I was told that in order to live a happy life as a black man with a gamut of nationalities running through my veins, I had to be the best. Being average as a black man would mean I would not make it to the top. I would say that that is far from the truth. Let's look at some of my sports heroes: Michael Jordan, Walter Payton, Marcus Allen, and many others who were cut when they started their sport. They worked extremely hard to become what we refer to as some of the "greatest in their games."

In one sense, many of the greats would have never been great if they weren't the worst first. I coached some awesome players and two of the best I had that went on to play professional sports were cut as well, when they first started their careers. The commonality to all of the people I worked with and my heroes was they had a driving force behind them, they actually never wanted to experience that feeling again.

When you were a child, you perceived and acted according to what you were told or not told. You moved through life as it came to you. You moved at the beat of the world around you, based on how others would lead you to believe it was to be. Once the world taught you to react in life, you did what was needed to survive, developing the new programs that are now driving you. This is where programs start to develop, as we protect ourselves from losing more of our connection to love. This is how it works, and now, because you know how to survive, you let your past drive your choices today.

Right now you can begin to understand how the Programs were created, and take a look at what is running you. So, what will you do? You can take ownership and move forward, or you can give the power to the memories or to the people who played a part in those times. It is a choice you may not have known you have until now. Are you ready to claim what you want, a clear present? It is your time to claim it all and move forward.

Keep the focus on yourself. Clean up what you can see about you and go forth. Know that when you point a finger at others, three fingers point back at you. So, what are those things you can clear up about yourself? The list may be long or short. Go for it. This is a great time to pause, put down your book, pick up your pen and paper, and let it flow.

STOP, LISTEN, and FEEL

STOP—no matter what it is you are carrying, let it all come up. LISTEN—to what is really happening now, not what you are carrying from the past. See how it is either here with you or not. FEEL—claim your power back. Be with what is really right in front of you now. What is in front of you at the moment? You are arriving at zero or nothing. It's time to start living from where you are in the present.

The past is often calling us to remind us of the Program we created to survive. I am often recalling the details of my life. I can recall so many moments that took place when I was with others. There are pictures of places that tie to my memories. Look at it, we actually see everything in pictures. Words like pictures are embedded into the Program we carry forward. We give power to our words that create the reality we see. Even these words you are reading now have formed pictures that have you connecting to what you know.

What if you change the meaning of the picture and the words? You would have created a new picture and a new meaning of the words. You now have the ability to create a new picture, give words new meaning, and change the experience of the memories to serve your highest good.

Yes, it can be this simple. You just have to allow yourself to believe and have faith. Let go, and let God.

Imagine if you were in the same moment, and had a different perspective. You could shift your life right in the moment. Have you ever seen a living Grinch? Have you stopped to think about what happened to create a Grinch around Christmas that brings joy to so many other people? What if someone had all they wanted for Christmas, yet there were arguments they overheard around money from their childhood. That deep pain and reaction to that experience forms the Program that can continue to run in the background of your life now. What if the picture was shifted and you were someone else in the same household? For whatever reason, you never saw or heard the arguments. The same picture would transform the experience of Christmas for you in every way going forward.

Let's look at how you change a memory in your mind. You are the one pulling up the pictures in your mind. This is where you have a choice. To give the pictures no meaning, you will have conquered the waves of emotion. You are free because you already let go in your mind. It is all up to you. It is the mental matrix that you have moved beyond. What will you do with it?

We are the ones creating the pictures. What will we do with the pictures and words we create?

What are we creating in the world around us? The mind is like a spider, weaving its world from inside of itself. The human race is connecting more and more in the same way. We are using the web of the internet to bring our world to us one thought at a time. That same invisible connection the spider has to the universe, is how we are using the web of the internet to bring our world to us one thought at a time. That is how.

All of life is determined by your connection.

What are we connecting to? What are we holding on to? Imagine we put everything we are attached to into a backpack. In life, we all have a backpack. As kids we put our homework in them, we put our notes to our parents, often our lunches. Whatever we have or have not, or may have needed, was in our backpacks. Now, if we have kept our backpack through life with us all this time, we would have accumulated so many things in this tiny backpack. Some things we did not even know were there. A big part of the backpack is not our stuff—it is our memories, our past, and our experiences. As we get older, our backpacks become the meanings we give our cars, our houses, and our other possessions.

Part of my transformation happened when we began our journey we referred to as "Peace Across America." It is what triggered us to live like minimalists in our lives today. In the spring of 2019, we left our house, sold most of our belongings, and as we hit the road we had most of what we needed in a couple of actual backpacks each. Every so often, we would clear them out. We would clear out the sand and clear out crumbs from lunch. Who knows what? What I realized is, if it were never cleared, the junk within would begin to smell. That is the backpack of your life you have now. It is beginning to smell.

Two options here: put it down and let it be cleared by another, such as God, or stop and clear it out yourself. It's time to get going with life.

I choose to clean up after myself.

Let's circle back. Identify, know the setbacks that are here with you.

STOP, LISTEN, AND FEEL

Somewhere a thought shows up. From a biological standpoint, our brain is moving faster than we are aware of. If we can align our conscious thoughts with where we are in our everyday lives, we can live our lives from the present.

Now, really think about this . . .

Every time we move, there is a thought attached to it, whether you are aware of it or not. In order to see the subtle thoughts, it is time to STOP the movements triggered by your unconscious thinking. STOP the extra movements, the fidgeting, and take some time to see what is presenting itself, so you can see the Program going on in your mind and running your life. LISTEN to see what you hear. Start to witness this for yourself. It is happening in the background, and it will run you until you hear it, identify it, and move forward. FEEL what is there. The subtle thoughts are triggering feelings, which are attracting into your life what you see today.

Just choose to let it all go, and then come forward. Practice these steps often and it will begin to transform your life fast. No one will know why your life is moving forward in such a grand way.

Is the Program stopping you or are you stopping yourself? You can be in forward movement, and if something comes up out of the blue, you get triggered. The Program can bring you to a complete and instant stop. Whether the Program is expected or not, its power can stop the strongest anytime.

Now we are getting into a deeper understanding of how the Program affects your operating system in life. Once you have this understanding, you can begin to make choices using STOP, LISTEN, and FEEL. Here you are, coming into a deeper awakening. What has shown up to be a great quality of those who evolve is tenaciousness. Stay at it until you identify the name for the Program that has been currently running your life. Now you have the space to recognize the Program and return to zero or nothing. Keep going and have the discipline to finish. Like when they were clearing Neo in *The Matrix*: first was the bug in the car; then another time was when he had to throw it all up.

We must get all of the echo programs out to fully let the light in. As we open up and become more clear, we are ready to move forward. Often we are looking at the echo of the original program, and we can get stuck there. Keep doing the work and dive in. Get clear, 100 percent clear. Until then we have yet to reach the Program. This is the nature of clearing. Remove all that is holding you back. Clearly release all distractions that take you out and occupy your presence. Your distractions are the subtle movements that keep you from seeing where your mind goes. Once you have gained the freedom to move consciously forward, you will have discovered a new sense of peace in your life.

Now that you have begun to clear through the SLF process, you will move faster and begin to connect and center. I call this the three Cs. **C**lear, **C**onnect, and **C**enter is the expansion of your evolution. Clear, as you allow your feelings to transform. Connect over and over to your highest and reach for what you see for your life. Get centered and organize your thoughts to allow the new programs to come forward. Only the light can do this. In order to see in the darkness of the unknown we must turn the light up. You will begin to see what is there with each positive point going forward. This is your chance to remove all of what no longer serves you, using the SLF process. We must see it all to reach full enlightenment. To bring the light fully in on the inside, it is up to you to turn your gaze in and find the zero point, and focus on our own heart. Remember, zero or nothing is the point inside of you where all is possible. When we clear the old-programs and reach the zero point within, we can then create a new present.

Now we are getting it. It's the Program that is creating the movie called your life. As you have begun to STOP, LISTEN, and FEEL you have started the remake to live the movie of your dreams. What we have been working with are the echo programs that have stemmed off the Program ruling your life. Let's keep going until we have gotten to the first program that caused you to disconnect from God.

Remember as you begin the three **C**s—Clear, Connect, and Center—you are writing the sequel of the movie called "Your Life." You see through your eyes only. Somewhere the thought is showing up, and you see through that lens. You are in a movie. Whatever that movie is for you, you are the main character. The movie called "Your Life" revolves around you. It is based on what your mind creates. Everyone else, your mother, your father, your sisters, your brothers, your friends, your teachers, your doctors, your enemies, everyone is a supporting cast member in the movie of your life. You are the director. You have chosen everyone else to play a role and they move around you. You are commanding them with no words needed. You are the producer bringing it all forward, producing every action, drama, comedy, you name it. You are the producer calling the shots.

You get all the credit, and now that you are willing to take the credit, you can guide this movie forward in the direction you wish to go. So, let's go; it is time to ride!

"Let's Ride!" song by Nahi
If you don't open your mind, you won't get it.

4 ESTABLISH A NEW PROGRAM & TRANSFORM YOUR LIFE.

I saw it, and I am sure many see it for themselves. I saw how my past connection to the Program was running my life. I saw how I spoke of wanting peace. I spoke of wanting love. In the end, I had misery and was missing the mark of finding peace and love. When we realize what we have is not aligned with what we say we want, then we can move forward to create the life we desire. When I came to grips with the fact that I wanted other things more in my life than peace and love, I recognized that my deepest desire was to stay in the comfort of what I knew. Then I entered a crossroad of choice. I could then make the choice to move forward or not. We now get to choose to stay in the pattern of our past or step into a new life.

Understand, if you are complaining about the drama someone brings in your life and it is still there, it is because somewhere inside you want it. Yes, you want it. If you wanted something else, you would choose to have it. It is really that simple: We can complain about others, or even how everything about the system is stacked against us. If we really don't want it, we will stop playing with it in every way possible.

When I am talking to people about the Program that is running their life, they often talk about how others have held them back. Most people then need to become willing to recognize *they* are the ones holding themselves back. You may be saying that it is someone else's fault. No, the truth is you have given the power to others to hold you back. Now that you have realized that you are the director of your life, you can move forward. Once I moved past my own limitations, I was able to start choosing to create consciously in my life.

At one point, I said to my staff I want to make a bigger impact for people who looked like me. So, we created a program called "Teach One, Reach One." It was the beginning program for "Yoga and Life Empowerment Teacher Training." To make sure I could help whomever I wanted, we created a scholarship program. We gave scholarships to those who live in lower economic cities and on reservations, to people who have been in domestic violence situations, and to veterans and their family members. We ended up with 44 people in the training. Twenty-two people paid and 22 had scholarships. This was the most diverse class we had. The impact is still causing waves in the world, because of the conversations around diversity. So many people have gone on to do powerful things in their community. This is what we all can do when we keep clearing the programs and the echo programs of what has held us stuck in our old life.

Establish a new way of being by creating what you desire in thought, and allow it to transform your life. Clean up your side of the street, and keep the focus on yourself. This is where the magic happens. If you allow your thoughts to continue in the same pattern of the Program, you will keep creating what you have.

He breathed the word, and all the stars were born.
~ PSALM 33:6

There it is. So, if your thoughts remain in the past, you will continue to live out the life that you have. When you shift your programs to a new place, you will gain access to something new. Keep cleaning the house. If you clean up one room, it is easy to see where the dirt is. So, move around and clean up the other room. To have a clean inner house, you keep going until it is all cleaned up. That is it. Clean it all up.

Just clean up your side. If someone else wants to, they will clean up their side. No need to wait—get going. All you have is today. Take ownership of your choices and move forward. You see what you do; others see what they do. The view they keep of you is where they are. I was told a long time ago, someone's thoughts and opinions of you are their own. It is also not your business to be concerned with the thoughts of others. We will always be able to make reasons for why we are stuck. Have no reasons to hold yourself stuck in the past programs.

I started this book and knew to what level I wanted to write. I knew that I wanted to write the best book possible. I knew if I told my family, I would be able to hold myself accountable to put pen to paper and get it all done. I also knew that it was possible that I may hear views I may not want. It was up to me to choose how I would react to what they may say. I chose to see everything from a new light versus from my old program. Now I would see from the Program of love as I embraced whatever was sent from the love they had for me. What I noticed was everyone was supportive, or at least kept their thoughts to themselves.

One statement I received was that my goal of this book becoming a *New York Times* bestseller was "great." It was suggested that writing this book should pull all the negative thoughts and life experiences out of me. Then I could put these experiences anchored in the Program behind me as I "sail into the sunset of life."

Well, to be honest, when I received the text message, my Program pulled some deep seeds up to the surface. Because of the way I saw it, I applied STOP, LISTEN, and FEEL until I could release it. I turned it around, and entered the program of peace and love. When you have a view or feeling from the old Program that doesn't support your direction, turn it around and see just what is available if you use the tools you now have. STOP, LISTEN, FEEL! Let go and let God do the work. Shed the fears and maybe a few tears. Release the layers of the echo programs and move on.

What is there to lose? You already have the dirt in front of you, playing out in your life. Do you want to keep the sticky mess? Do you want to keep fighting? Do you want to be right, or are you ready to be happy? Do you want to be right, or do you want to find peace? Find your programs that support your highest good and move forward. The work to be done is an inside job. If you always have to be right, you will lose many sweet moments of life. To live the life of your dreams, this is it, do the work.

You are the one who is carrying the problem forward. The fight is in you. STOP, LISTEN, FEEL, and CLEAR. Let it move through. My dad once said it takes "two to fight and one to have peace." I sit with this often and let myself have the peace I desire within.

So, what is it going to be?

Many people have the Program running in their heads of the fear of what others are thinking and doing. Yes, there are people doing things that are far less than what we know can be done in the world. They are operating from the negative, killing, shaming, abusing, being racist, trafficking, performing evil acts in the world. What makes you think that they know how to do something different than what they are doing? Playing the judge is far from what it is about. Jesus said, "Let thou without sin cast the first stone." Just live out the teachings of the ancient ones, and let it go. This is about moving forward.

As you clear, all will follow from there. The earth is a body, the body that houses all of us as one. When you look at your body, you likely have arms and legs, feet, hands, organs, intestines, a head, and more. No need to cut off your nose to spite your face, if you are upset about what is going on in the world. Clean it up, be the solution. We can all clear this body; we can all clear earth's body when we clear. STOP—know what you have. LISTEN—hear it, see it—and FEEL. What are you carrying forward? We can put it down and move forward. Do you want to keep the Program? If so, that is okay. It must be serving something you wish to keep. You can also choose to let it go. So, when you are ready, let's put it down. FEEL the lightness. Let's ride into the sunset of life.

There is a story of one of our trainees that was stuck in her old Program, the Program that held her family back for years. One thing Freddy went through was letting go of this feeling and the thoughts of not being wanted. She had been through plenty of things from her childhood from both of her parents.

What was interesting to see was my partner and I had been going through our patterns for years. A totally different space, yet parent issues nonetheless. We run a Program; it attracts to us what fits our Program, and we can clean it all up. This is how it works. People come together to reflect on each other's movie of their lives. Freddy's parents had split early in her life. She was willing to clear up the echo programs of her life. As Freddy cleared, everyone in the training had an opportunity to clear what was reflected in their lives simultaneously, so we all could move forward. This is a critical understanding of how we are always watching our movie, and what is taking place on the outside is happening on the inside. When one person clears, others have the opportunity to clear their lives as well.

Freddy had been through a lot and here was a chance to release a layer of her Program.

Freddy was running several programs from each parent. When one program would taper off, another would kick in and be masked by the other echo programs. Freddy would often feel like she was the mother at home. She would take care of her mom whenever her mom would drink at night. Then came the 16 years she had not seen her dad. So many programs were built around her disconnection from her parents.

Freddy came to Empowerment Training and committed to doing the work and letting go of the need to tell her mom what to do. She started with letting go of the need to fix her mom. Two days later, after removing the patterns she used to defend herself and justify her actions, Freddy's mom contacted her and said she would be gone when she came home, as she was checking herself into rehab.

That was the proof Freddy needed. The proof to clean up her side of the street. The proof that doing the work on herself may be the chain reaction to an instant shift for herself and in her relationships.

It is all a heartbeat away.

The next layer to clear came in the Program of her relationship with her father. It was time for Freddy to reach out to her dad, the one she had not spoken to in 16 years. She chose to see beyond all the reasons they were estranged. She called, and he picked up the phone and immediately said, "I have been waiting sixteen years for this call." After training, she called him again that night. They talked into the wee hours of the night. When she returned to training, she was so pumped she forgot about being tired, as her connection was on overdrive. They both wanted this connection so much that after training, her dad flew her out to see the other part of her family, and a new program began to emerge.

That is how it works. You do the work. You use your tools of STOP, LISTEN, and FEEL. You shift your connection, and doors open to strengthen that connection. Where can you go now? Be willing to STOP—see where you are now. LISTEN—to how you are responding from a new program. FEEL—as you center yourself into a new program, and consciously choose to start a new life.

You will move through seven opportunities to embrace your new programs, a series of tests unconsciously created by you as you direct your life to a new way of being. To embrace your new program, you will identify what you desire to bring into your new life. As the new program is activated by you with conscious choice, you will create a new operating system. Now is your time to be an active participant in creating your life.

Reflection

STOP: Take a moment to see what is showing up for you. Are you relating to anything here for yourself? What are you seeing that is no longer serving you? What are the patterns in your life that are showing up?

LISTEN: What are the Programs driving you today? See the thoughts that are showing as dreams.

FEEL: Deep down, what do you feel when these thoughts come up? Remember it is up to you, and what you do with your thoughts. You are writing your movie called *Your Life*. What are the programs you want to carry forward? How do you want your life to look in the future?

5 CLEAR OUT THE PATTERN DEFAULTS.

For many years I have had an operating system default. I removed one of the strongest ones before it left me in a place of feeling alone. It all stemmed from a moment in my childhood, a moment where I felt I was right. Since I was not acknowledged for the way I felt and how I wanted to be treated, I took on the Program that said "I was right." The Program would play out in my life as a need to always be right. I would sometimes hurt others in my close relationships, in order to prove I was right to myself. The Program that was running me at the time was not serving me at my highest, which for me meant a time to transform and find the Program that will best serve my life in the present.

As you look at the Program, it is important to recognize the operating system defaults, and STOP to see where you go when things move in a negative direction. Remember, this is your life and yours alone. Put down the blame and reclaim your flame. You are the only one who can clear yourself. This is your work.

When we clear out the old, we will begin to uncover the peace within. The peace within is a stream of wellness inside of us all. Tap in and let it flow. Like a beaver creates a dam, we can create blocks within ourselves as well. The dam a beaver builds can trap fish, they can hang out, and even get comfortable. Remove the blocks, and let it flow in your life.

"I'll be damned."

If you have been around long enough, that old saying, "I'll be damned," may have been said a time or two from those in your life. No need to be damned; it's just time for a new program. Take the time, watch your language, and choose to create magic in your life.

I have always found it interesting that we are taught to spell, and what not to say. The focus has been on the process of spelling rather than the impact of the words. If you think about the concept of spelling as casting a spell, you will see how we have often created darkness in the world. As we open up to consciously choosing our words, we can create magic in our lives, the lives of others, and in our world.

As you do the work, you get to choose how it is going to be. It can be hard. It can be easy. It is a choice. There is no "hard" unless you choose to create the Program to fit the words "it is hard." You are the one who gets to make your reality. The "easy way" is just a perspective you can choose. By allowing "easy" to be the Program of choice, you have shifted your life in a different direction. It is all a choice. STOP, evaluate, LISTEN, know, FEEL, and choose wisely.

What do you do when a pattern comes up? STOP, know yourself, study *you*. We talked about listening; put it into practice. LISTEN, deeply, and it starts with hearing *you*. What thoughts are taking place in the background? When you hear them, they come to the foreground and can be cleared. FEEL the thoughts, and let them go.

Remember we cannot see our own face. It may be time to ask a friend what they see of you. Only ask when you are ready to LISTEN. Maybe sit down, play chess, and LISTEN between the moves. Drink some hot, hot tea, so you have to sip your tea and LISTEN.

Know thyself and to thy own self be true!
~ William Shakespeare

You have many tools to use to learn about you. Let your breath be your teacher. See where you can give and receive. See how your breath moves. Is it short or long? Hold your breath in. What do you feel? Hold your breath out. What do you feel? You will notice how holding your breath in, eventually you must breathe out. Same happens when you hold your breath out, and you must eventually breathe in. See how you must give and receive. You can learn this through your breathing.

> Go deeper than your thoughts. It is all right here for you to awaken to.

Here is a personal reflection I want to share to help you see it is up to you to choose what you want your life to look like. My story of intimate relationships has been vast. I have been married three times and had a relationship for eight years where we moved as if we were married. Because I had a pattern of looking for the perfect connection in relationships, it meant I would not find the perfect relationship, because I was still in a space of "looking." I had said I wanted to renew our vows at ten years, so I could recommit and go deeper. I was in my first marriage for nine years and nine months. My thoughts continued to create the miss. This was birthed by my childhood Program, "there has to be a better way."

That was the miss; I was looking for what I was missing, because I was in fear of what I had seen in the past. The Program I was running was "looking for love." I wasn't seeing where I could have been creating a new program, called "love is in my life." My old Program I was running would start with someone in my life—and I already knew in my unconscious mind that I would see them as not capable of being the love I wanted, because of the Program running my life. I unconsciously knew, at some point, I would want to leave, no matter what. I had to see beyond the Program I was running. When I was ready to see what was in me, I would see beyond it. I had not yet **stopped** and gotten still. I had not **listened** to myself and **felt** what I wanted unconsciously was to keep my old Program going because I felt safe in the familiar.

I went into my second marriage and there it was again. It all came to the surface even faster. I had to look in, to release my hurt. I was blessed, as when I was ready to begin to release playing in the Program, she packed half of the house and left from my reality.

Both marriages had started from a foundation that would no longer serve me. I was looking to see beyond the Program of the racism that was triggered in my marriages. Then there was the Program of my age. I needed to see beyond the programs others were running and how they were interacting with my own Programs.

That is when I was able to shift. There were a series of programs running, to move forward from. Once I had seen my Programs more clearly, it was time for me to go deeper and to see how others have Programs that can pull me backwards or propel me forward. It was up to me how I played in the dance. Once I chose to take responsibility, it all cleared up.

Then came another relationship that triggered me. This time I slowed down and really looked at it. I began to see how I was the common denominator in all my relationships. I had to step back and look at how my relationships were reflecting my hurt within. You see, I was carrying a vibration that was attracting the same life patterns to me. Everything would start with a view of things being good, yet there were difficult moments that could have been viewed differently and that would have established a different foundation. I was the one with the Program running, and I had to see it, stay or walk away, and transform it into a new reality. It would never matter what her program was, nor matter what relationships she witnessed, or how she was in the past. That was not mine to shift. I was ready to shift my desire to run and look for love in some other situation.

I needed to let go of seeing my partner as my problem; the Program could keep running in our lives if either of us kept playing in the negative. If there was a problem for her, she would need to clear her program. I had to go in and find my Program, and after contemplating for three years I became clear what was holding me back from love. I let go of seeing the judgement I had on myself. Because I had recognized my Program, I could stop feeling guilty and allow others to attack me to cover their Program. What that meant for me was to go deeper, go deeper and remove the self-hate, so that I could love me 100 percent. That is the practice of self-love.

After each relationship, if I was going to be able to have love again, I was going to have to connect to a deeper state of love. So that's what I did. I looked at the blows and the attacks as signs to love myself more and keep moving. I knew what it could look like to connect to love and have love as my new program. Beyond the judgements of age, beyond racism, beyond the differences, I went into the program of self-love, to make that connection with the one waiting for me, my highest self. I was the one who would love me, no matter the circumstance. It was all about me, not good or bad, right or wrong; it just is.

Once I knew myself, I was ready to move forward into love as my new program. I would open up to love and let "her" in. By knowing who and what in your life you have created, and by clearing your old Programs, you will begin to know your dream life is here, now. I had to see the good and the bad of it all. I recognized it as all good, because I realized it will all move me forward if I allow it to do so.

Growing up, I saw my uncle as one of the happiest people I knew. So, I took some of those traits and brought them forward. As I shifted, I recall knowing I wanted to be the example my kids could see, and if they chose to, they could choose a program to evolve their lives for the better. Once that awareness came forward, it was time to be present and move on. Live full on, full steam ahead.

Observe how, as you release, the path is getting clearer. Where do you want to go from here? Shine light on it. Get clear. If there are things you don't like, there are things you do like. Know them. Own them. The clearer the pictures of your life, the easier you will remember how you desire to live.

Let's go back to Freddy's story. There was a default Program she was living with around her dad, "he doesn't care for me." One day she reached out because she wanted to go and see him and her family again. He did not answer her call or email for a couple of days. I recall her coming into my office and saying she was upset and couldn't work. She had been reaching out to her dad, and he never returned her call.

So, I was listening and asked, "Would you like to hear a possibility?"

Freddy said, "Yes."

I replied with, "Okay, stay with me for a moment. Both of your parents are in the military, correct?"

"Yes", said Freddy.

"Let's say your dad is on a top-secret mission and he is out in the mountains, with no reception. You know, like a James Bond, 007-type or Ethan Hunt in *Mission Impossible*.

She smiled and went with it.

I continued, "So what if he is just in a space where he has not gotten your messages?"

Still upset and yet, Freddy had a new perspective. Freddy said, "I am going to go to lunch and will come back."

As soon as the door shut, I heard it reopen. I knew it was her. Freddy walked back in my office and said, "You aren't going to believe this."

"I am sure I will," I replied.

Freddy responded, "My dad just got back to me. He texted me and said he was off where there was no reception, and as soon as he could he would contact me. It should be in a couple of hours."

We laughed, and Freddy went to lunch.

That is how clearing your Programs can work. See the old patterns show up, use SLF, and consciously choose a new place to go.

Create new habits that support the new program you will live from going forward. When we shift our train of thought, we open up to all of the wonder that is available.

Keep going. There is more to Freddy's story.

Reflection

STOP: What are you learning about yourself? Are you seeing the Program? Are you ready to move forward?

LISTEN: What do you call the Program? What is the name? How is it working in your life?

FEEL: Now go forward and watch. Allow yourself to go deeper and be a disciple of what you want in life. Now is the time to choose what you want to bring forward.

6 BRING NEW PEOPLE TO THE TABLE.

No matter where we are, life continues to move ahead. My life began to move forward the closer I got to the root of the Program that was running me. I observed, as things began to progress with Liz and me. I moved into a different vibration. I took Liz with me to the music studio to meet my producer, Jamie. It was great to be able to see how others saw us, especially since Jamie had seen for years what was going through my life. We went in, and Liz was able to sit in as we laid down vocal tracks. Something many may know when doing music is, it can take several hours just to get a first version of a song. Liz went outside to make a phone call. Then Jamie said, "Hey, I like her. You all are good together. So, do you want to know my take?"

"Sure," I said.

"Well, you have been a serial monogamist and that is okay, if you want to live life like that. Or you can see that what you have is great and go for it, love deeper and more fully than ever before."

The echo of my Program was already exposed, and here it is, at the start of my relationship, a chance to choose and move forward. Sometimes even a coach needs a coach, and in that moment, that was exactly what I needed to hear.

Now you have uncovered a Program(s) that, when removed, will allow you to achieve your next level of connection. Take a moment to STOP. LISTEN: what do you want? What is it you will put in front of all else to achieve it? Maybe it is vast, like world peace. If so, you must start where you are. Go for the new program, wherever you are. Implement it right where you are now. FEEL: as it expands beyond when it is time.

Your Programs brought what you have wanted over and over. It brought what you have focused on, ahead of all else in life. Yes, I know you may say I am not interested in the jerks I have in my life. Let's look at that. If they are there, then yes, you really do want them around. You want them, because if you did not want it or them, whatever that is would be gone.

There is no magic pill, there is no magic diet. The place to get honest with yourself is: What do you want? What are you willing to give up to get to the connection you want in your life? If you do not want something in your life, you wouldn't have it. If you don't want it, STOP continuing to play with it. Pause, hold on. Get clear on what you want. LISTEN to *you*, at the depth of the silence inside, and know it, taste it, smell it, and FEEL it. Get all of your senses involved, and allow it to come forward. It is time to let it in.

Understand what is taking place at the core of your being. What would it feel like if you lived your dream and dropped the nightmare you have carried forward? Let go of the need to please others; that is their job for themselves. Those who love you will be happy, as you find your own way. When someone loves you, and they know happiness is there for you, they will rejoice in your happiness. It is really that simple.

As you go further, begin to build the world you want, in thought first. Who would you have around you? What do you want? Sit down and ask yourself these questions. Be honest with yourself. How would they treat you if they were loving you in your life? As you are having a conversation, is there a particular way they would listen? When you are down, would they know or even stop and care? Would they reach out to you if you stopped reaching out to them? Know the relationship and how they would stand for you. Is it how you would stand for them or want to be treated?

How would your friend greet you when you come together? The love is in the details, and so is the devil. Which one do you want to live with?

The ones you want around, know how they will respond to the small growing moments. When the giant moments come forward, how will they show up? Know this, as this is a great reflection of how you stand for yourself in the moments of your life. When there is a conflict on the outside or a negative moment, shift to seeing the Program within that is running this moment. That is your growing edge.

It took some time for me to know what I wanted in my relationship at home. What I can say from where I am in my relationship with my wife is that we hold each other in deep care. I see Liz celebrate my small and large victories. Because I know how it feels and how I desire to feel, I stand for her in the same way. It is a major shift I made in my life. Because I know what I want, I am able to bring a different version of myself forward to love all the people in my life. I see others become love in my life and in the life of others, as well. I even see it in the people I don't know on the street, in a simple smile and gesture of kindness. I am also aware of the relationships I have had to let go of, as we are no longer moving in the same direction.

It's not right or wrong, good or bad; it just is. It is a choice based on how I want my life to be as I move forward.

What is good for the goose is good for the gander.

Let's take a moment and ask some questions to go further into what you want in your life.

STOP: see what is present.

LISTEN: What does support look like? When you fall back and can use a loving hand, will they know? Will they care? When you are nervous or scared, what will it look like? Can you be the support for yourself, so you can be that support for others?

FEEL: It is time to allow your team to hold you up in life, so you can do the same for those you love and live into your greatness. You and God can be the greatest teammates. Let the All Mighty hold you up. It is time to treat yourself with the love you desire from others. Treat yourself with the love you give to others.

There is a coach's saying, 'It is easy to slow down a thoroughbred, it is dang near impossible to speed up a donkey."

It is easy to slow down, yet it is harder to speed up. Give yourself lots of love. Is your mind running like a wild colt or being stubborn when it comes to recognizing how to love and support yourself? A wild colt is powerful, free, plays and dances through life, and dances with love and abundance. A donkey is strong, stubborn, and moves only when ready. Know that all you have to do is give a donkey a little love and guidance and it will plow any field you ask it to. No matter where you are, make the connection, and watch what a great harvest you can have in the end.

You can choose to be the love in your life. You can consciously choose to surround yourself with a team of thoroughbreds and/or donkeys to fit what is appropriate in your life today.

Purge to Surge.

Look around and take inventory. What can you let go of? Who or what is holding you back from connecting to the greatest life? There is a technique called the *release technique*. It was discovered by a man who was a multi-millionaire, who was given only a few weeks to live. He went to the mountains of Sedona, Arizona, to live out his final days. When he would go outside and sit to reflect, he would see such amazing sights. In Sedona, you don't watch the sun rise or set. You watch the mountains opposite the sun, and you turn to see the beautiful colors that pop out as the sun hits them. You can tell who lives there and who doesn't, because of the way they face. It is hard for those who are sun-gazers to imagine turning away from the sun at first. Then, when they see the colors and the beauty the light can bring forward, it takes their breath away.

Back to the man and the release technique: As the days passed, it dawned on him that he should give away his stuff. Why would he need a jet, helicopter, several cars, and other stuff if he was going to die? He did not have family to leave it to, so he found people who could benefit from what he had. He found plenty of people to help and take the load off his hands. He lived beyond the time predicted for his life to end.

The more he released, the better he felt. So much time had passed that when he went to see his doctor, all the doctor could do was welcome him, and ask where he had been. The doctor thought his patient had gone off and lived the best life he could, and passed away. The doctor wanted to know what he had been doing because he looked great. He told the doctor, and the release technique was birthed.

What do you need to release to open up to something new? In my life, I have lived it all and was ready to own freedom as a new program. In April of 2019, my wife and I sold everything in our house and hit the road. Thirty-four paintings were sold or given away. Furniture, video games, books, dishes, clothes, shoes, beds—you name it. We were told how hard it was to watch us give away good stuff.

Immediately when we packed the car, closed the doors, and said our goodbyes, I felt free. The pains in my body left. We journeyed to see how we could live life with our newfound freedom. How could we live life, full-on, and maintain this level of happiness and joy? We were cutting cords by letting all of our stuff go. We were becoming minimalists and getting free.

One person's trash is another person's treasures.

It is an incredible practice to release all of what is tethering you to the past. Take it on; try a 30-day purge to surge. Start with this: Over the next 30 days, get rid of one thing a day. See how it feels. Get yourself unstuck. It may include releasing some people in your life who continue to hold you to the past; or it may include behaviors, attitudes, beliefs, or belongings. Make a list, numbered 1 to 30, and write down what you'll get rid of. After you get rid of your item, take your time and see what comes up internally. Put it on the list and notice the Program that is attached. Know what leaves your body as you let the item, person, or whatever move on. When it is time, say your goodbyes with an open heart, and move forward with forgiveness, compassion, and peace.

The process of letting go is incredible. Let freedom become a new program for you. I met a lady whose mom every year would have them as kids give away their favorite item to a friend or a stranger. She first tried as a kid giving her stuff to her siblings, thinking that if it were close by, she would be able to play with it, see it, and feel better. She recalled how when she saw her brother playing with her stuffed animal, she learned quickly that the more she could not see the item, the better she felt. You know" out of sight, out of mind.

What I noticed about her was that she was one of the most free people I had ever encountered. Choose it for yourself. Be free, be at peace, be in love because you want to. That may mean letting go so you can have room for those you want to take a seat at the table with you.

When you are ready to let go, you will understand that sometimes you have to commit to something new. When you are in a pattern that continues to come up, sometimes it is best to pause and just go in another direction.

Let's see what it looks like to head in another direction.

Reflection

STOP: See just what is it you are holding on to. What is the pattern that is showing up over and over again?

LISTEN: What can you release that holds you to the past?

FEEL: What do you want to feel like as your life unfolds? Are you willing to let it in?

7 ESTABLISH A NEW ROUTINE AND PUT IT INTO ACTION.

While we were on the road, we found a groove that worked for us. So much that we would live it pretty steadily, moving around from city to city with a sense of ease, while living in our world of just the two of us. During our stops, we would regroup and find a new flow. Then we would shift when we were on the road again. It became a natural flow based on each moment. It was an interesting flow to be in, free of what the world was experiencing, and living it in our own way. We knew that to be the most centered in life, we would eventually learn to live in the flow, no matter where we were, on the road or stationary. We began to live the lessons we had learned on all levels.

We can move with our new program when we gain access to the flow of life and move with ease consciously, from one moment to the next. Take some time today to see how your mind moves and how you think throughout your day. See just how the Program is running in your head. There is a pattern that will move you in familiar moments. In the *Yoga Sutras* by Patanjali, the asana portion of yoga is used as a tool to still one's mind. It is up to each of us to see how the world is playing out in our thoughts. By bringing our mind to stillness and clearing our thoughts, we can see just how we are connected within the matrix or sea of life. From this point, we can again meet and be in a relationship with God. It is the matrix that is moving you when you are unconscious, and because you are living unconsciously, it has you. Be willing to break free. To understand another, you have to walk a mile in his shoes. To understand yourself, you must be present as you walk a mile in your own shoes. Consciously move forward.

What shifts can you make to move forward from here? Clear it all out. See into the dark spaces of your soul. When you clear out a refrigerator, you will see just how much room there is. You get to choose what to fill it up with. This is the point you are coming to now, and you get to choose what to put into your soul. Discipline is the key to finish and get to the Program you desire to live from. Get all the way to the "Zero Point," the zero or nothing that will allow you to move forward and live the life of your dreams.

It is easy to feel happiness, peace, or love for a moment. It takes discipline to continue to move with a new program. Make a commitment to yourself. Know you have the discipline because you choose to. It is time to move forward.

What tools do you have or need to move forward? It's time to STOP the old and choose to live this as your best life. This book is a tool, use it often. Yoga may be a tool you use, to consciously move through your practice and see where your operating system is carrying you. Meditation is a tool. Learn to LISTEN to your mind and allow your life to be your meditation practice. FEEL the ease as you find the discipline to bring forward the connection to what you want.

Let it all set in and carry you forward. Let's uncover your way to communicate with the most high supreme. It has a lot of names, yet there is only one start to all of this as we know it. Whatever you want to call, it is great. Develop a relationship with it. You can start right now. Use your imagination. Imagine there is something. What would you do with a new best friend? Say "hi," and introduce yourself.

"Hi, my name is ____, and I am glad to meet you." Start there and keep going.

Now, take it another step. Know this: there are two parts to communication. There is listening and there is speaking.

Listen twice as much as you speak.

You were given two ears and one mouth. Yes, listen twice as much as you speak. To speak to God, you pray. To listen to God, you meditate. Start there, speak, ask questions, share *you*, and have gratitude. Now, listen and wait for a response. It can be that simple.

I have a prayer I use that I want to share with you. This is a prayer that came to me after hearing many amazing people speak and communicate with God in their way. I sat and asked God to grant me the words that would help all who read this have a prayer that would serve them best in the world today. Here is a prayer for you to connect deeper in your transformation today. (Aho) is a Native American term for "thank you.")

The Prayer of Connection.

(Sid McNairy)

> *Mother and Father of all, God, the infinite source, always was, always is, always will—beyond space, time, and form, the everlasting, the great mystery within us all, prime source, great spirit, creator—I call to you.*

Please forgive me for all the moments I have missed the mark. Please help me forgive all who have brought harm and dis-ease in my path. Please forgive all humans from the past and in the future for eternity, in all ways. Aho.

May I find a deep peace within that knows all is cared for by you, that all you have brought forward is sacred for my evolution. May my fellow humans feel the same. Aho.

May I find acceptance for all that has come to be and for what was, what is, and what will be, for there lies the deepest love of all. Aho

May I receive your blessings of abundance in the physical, spiritual, and in love in every way, while my fellow humans receive the same. Amen.

From the eyes of compassion, may you keep my heart strong and focused on your most high for me and my fellow humans. May we see peace, unity, and love while I help others do the same. Amen.

I am grateful for receiving the love from the most high.

I love you, Father. Thank you for loving me.

Thank you, thank you, thank you, God. Amen. Aho.

Now that you have started to communicate with the source of all, continue to bring forward clear and concise language to what you desire. Whatever you need to say, bring it forward. Take the time to meditate and LISTEN.

We have four pillars in our meditation system; let's look at the foundational tools: stillness, breath, connection, "no mind," and intuition. As you move through these five meditation tools, be still for 3-7 breaths before you move forward from each cue to breathe. Come into a deep state of stillness, be more still than ever before. Every time you come to meditate, become more still. This will allow you to truly witness where your mind goes.

****Be still for 3-7 breaths****

Let's get into the depth of your breath. Come into the awareness of your natural breath. Simply notice how your breath is moving in and out of your body. Let it move through and see it, go deep into it. Notice your breath for several minutes.

****Be still for 3-7 breaths****

Now, start your awakening breath. Breathe in for a steady four count, feel the pause on the fifth count. Then out for a four count, pause on the fifth count, and repeat. Do this seven times.

Then, let's move into your heart space. Once you have connected to your heart, feel your heartbeat. Take it all in. By going to your heart before taking note of what is going on in your mind, you will establish access to love and compassion. By going to your heart first, you will remove the obstacle of being consumed by the power of your earth self.

****Be still for 3-7 breaths****

Through the meditation practice, now observe as you go into a space of "no mind." Go in and observe as you take your inner gaze to your forehead center. Be in observation, "no mind," just be present. The practice of "no mind" is to awaken to what is being created. See your thoughts, free of judgement, just observe. See into the gap between your thoughts. Let that space grow one breath at a time.

Understand *you*; see it all with no judgements. Just see it move; see the patterns that show the reactions that come to the surface, your emotions that come forward, and your thoughts that move through. How is your mind creating, based on your understanding of you?

****Be still for 3-7 breaths*
*(free meditation on SidMcNairy.com)****

So much can come from us in this new space of listening. The new depth of creation within is key. Let's get to the zero point; this is the foundation where miracles can happen. This is where you are the magician of your life. Dream big, and move outside of the box you have put yourself in.

Let's look back at Freddy's story: As you can see, sometimes we just need another person's vantage point. Freddy's story unfolded with some major magic. Freddy had done so much work; she let go of the old and opened up so much. It began to touch all of her family members. When her mom returned from rehab, Freddy had grown by leaps and bounds, so much that Freddy's mom wanted to share her joy for Freddy's transformation. Her mom began to communicate with her nana, who responded with, "Well, why don't you contact your dad?"

This caused Freddy's mom to stop in her tracks. Nana said, "Call your dad."

Freddy's mom questioned, "Wait, how? My dad has been dead for forty years."

Nana responded, "No, he isn't dead. I said he was dead to you."

Now, imagine this: how would a child feel knowing her dad was dead? How would an adult live, moving through life with that same awareness? Alcohol may be the way they escape the pain of not having a dad. It could go as far as wanting to leave earth or becoming angry with God. Then imagine finding out your dad is not dead.

Freddy's mom made contact with her dad and began a healing process just before a major shift would touch them all. A week later, they were all by his bedside. Three generations of women had closure to a chapter that was being passed along. The work Freddy was willing to do caused a healing that all would be able to take on.

All of life is determined by your connection.

Understand it, see it, live it. This is where the magic is. The truth is, "All of life is determined by your connection." The more this sets in, the more you move into a creative connection through the life you have and the one you wish to live. Go in and gain access to living the life of your dreams.

Reflection

STOP: See you, see how you spend your day. Be willing to break free. See what you are holding on to and if it needs to be released.

LISTEN: Understand the impact of the Program, the voice running in the background.

FEEL: See what feelings you are holding on to, or what has you in a holding pattern. There's nothing to do, just let go, and move forward.

8 FIND THOSE TO WALK WITH.

There are moments when everyone can use a helping hand. My journey with Sam Brand began when I was coaching football, and he was playing basketball. I was also a college instructor at Morgan State University. Sam took my class, and little did I know, Sam said to himself, "The day I become a head coach, I am going to find Coach Sid, when that time comes, and get him to work with our guys."

The day Coach Brand called me, I had just finished a conversation with a friend who thought it would do my soul good to volunteer to help the youth in Baltimore. Coach called and told me how they had lost a player to gun violence in the city. He said he needed help and wanted to talk about what it would cost to get me there. I said, "Let's not talk about money. When we are done, all I want is a ring."

Initially, the players would come to my wellness center and take my yoga class. Just by being present they were shifting all the while, impacting me and the community. I could see that the connection we were sharing was elevating all of our programs.

I loved working with the Poly Technical High School Basketball Program, and we were winning from the foundation that was laid. Soon, we became champions on and off the court. We were coming off of the first of three state championships and were looking at how we could improve. Players were getting better, relationships were growing. I offered to watch Coach Sam on the court, to see what I observed. We had a great friendship, and I might see something that could help him improve his impact with the players on and off the court. As I watched several practices, I began to see the style of coaching that led to early wins. I noticed how one player was being coached harder because of his great potential. What was being missed was that, as they turned to coach the other players, this player would turn away, hold his head down, and would get down on himself. I noticed this and offered a new possibility to the coaching staff that would go on to help all. A few days later, this same kid was about to take his life, and it was caught because there was a new awareness. This player would go on to be a great leader and go on to play basketball after high school. Sometimes, even a coach needs a coach.

Let's roll it back a bit. Time to dive in, you cannot see your own face. Well, that is a true statement, unless you have a mirror. Let's look at two mirrors of choice in this case. A coach and an accountability buddy—people that can be in your life with different vantage points, to help you move forward.

You may have initial resistance to listening to another person's feedback. To get into full empowerment, you may just need a coach to elevate beyond what you cannot see. Often we will overlook what is taking place in the moment. We can all go on autopilot, missing the reactions we have created to protect ourselves from the pains from the past, the old Programs.

What would it look like for you to have a coach, to have a coach who only wanted you to reach your mountain top? To have a coach that just wanted you to live life fully?

As a coach, I loved my players. I still do. I especially loved those who gave their best effort and did the work. Many of my players played at their best of their abilities because they trusted I was helping them become the best player and person they could possibly become. The key is the trust. Find a coach you trust. Give way to what is there for the greatest work to be done.

Know that your coach is there to help you see what you have missed, to get you to live the life of your dreams. If you knew the problem, you would have already been where you want to be. Pick a coach who has the discipline to stay present to what is at hand. My ability to stay present for life helps me to be there for all who are ready to reach deep inward and live from their highest. I love seeing people elevate and be the way for others. These are the qualities you want when looking for a coach for yourself or your kids.

Would you ask someone who doesn't have the tools for directions to a place they have never been? No, you wouldn't. The best way to get to where you are headed is to ask someone who has the tools or has been there before. You will have to have faith and trust that, no matter how your coach received their information, it is all good. Just grab the lessons along the way and keep moving. No judgement needed, keep going forward.

Listen to know what you don't know. Receive feedback with an open heart. Feedback out of love will allow you to know how you are landing in the world. I love my coaches and how I am here because my life coaches have empowered me to be me. That is it. You can only be yourself, and there is a gift inside of you waiting to be birthed.

Find your coaches and your teammates for the life you want to be living. Your accountability buddies are your teammates and your friends in life that keep you on track. Love looks like letting you know when you have mud on your face. I was once with a teacher who had a big snot booger hanging out of her nose. I really did not want to say anything. I tried rubbing my nose as a signal, to no avail. I tried everything possible, even asking if I could have a tissue, anything to help without saying what was actually there.

Nothing was picked up. Finally, we were leaving after our session had completed. I had a choice to tell her or let her go into the next session with the booger hanging out of her nose. I chose to tell her. She grabbed that booger out and flicked it into her kitchen. Whoa. It was an interesting moment. Yet it was done.

I bring people in my corner that will love me enough to tell me with compassion when I have mud on my face. It is up to me to be willing to receive the love in the message, to evaluate what has been given, and move forward.

As you continue to move forward, reclaim your power by being accountable for your life. The best way to allow someone to help you is to bring them in as an accountability buddy, and invite them to be direct. To bring someone into the fold, you must be willing to listen and be honest with yourself, to uncover what was there in the past that got you to this point. Be willing to drop the echo programs. Know and trust who you are sharing yourself with, so that love can shine through. Often it is best to find someone willing to do the work on themselves, as well, so you can support each other. Let them know where you have been and where you want to go. Now let the work set in.

Early on in my life, I was fortunate to have coaches all around me and teammates who all wanted to win championships—which meant I had to also champion life. When I was coaching football at Northern Illinois University, I was coaching with a bit of a chip on my shoulder. I had experienced racism and affirmative action coming into coaching. I felt everywhere I turned, I had to prove myself. I was living in a mental space that was as competitive as you can imagine. I remember getting up bright and early to get in the gym, with my fellow coach who was my roommate, because our wives had not moved to town yet. He was a machine that way, and it helped me to work out harder so I could stay at my best. I will always have love for Coach Hagen, as I grew with him for many years to come. That same competitive space I had in the gym, I carried with me into the office. Being the youngest on the staff, I often wanted to prove myself, and it would get heated in the "war room" as many coaches call it. The coaches' meetings were intense, and meetings would go into the wee hours of the night. If I saw something that I thought wasn't going to work on any given play, I would say things with a lot of passion. It took me a long time to understand how others thought a powerful voice meant that anger was happening, especially from the Program that many see a black person coming from.

One day our head coach, Coach Novak, pulled me into his office. He asked, "Sid, have you seen yourself in the room?"

I thought to myself, *what does he mean?*

He continued, "When you get into it with some of the coaches, you may have a fight."

In my head I thought, *have you ever seen me fight?* As if I was thinking, *I wish they would.*

He then said, "You have these looks, that if I was them, I would want to fight you as well."

I thought, *I have no clue what he is saying.*

When I looked up, I felt furious. Coach said, "There it is, that look. I know you are a good guy, and that look gives away your power. Everyone knows exactly what you are thinking, and it's not good. People will be able to control you from that space."

Because Coach had pointed this out to me, I had a new level of peace, and I began to see myself in so many new ways. Even a coach needs a coach.

That is what a coach and your accountability buddy can provide in your life. Find the people you know, the ones you can drop your guard with—the people you can count on to stand by you, those who live far beyond everyday gossip. Find the people you can count on, no matter what is going on—the people you can count on when all else fails.

Take your time, and be gentle with yourself. Depending on your life experience, it may seem tougher for you than others to let people in. Evaluate what you want, ask questions, and be honest with those you want support from.

One of the greatest things a parent can do for their child is to get to know their coaches before signing them up for a sport or activity. Many programs in life can be built around the experience a kid has with coaches on teams. In one moment, a coach can break or shape a kid to reach their highest in every way.

The same can be said for you, as you make this level of transition and transformation of working with coaches and accountability buddies. When you choose to open yourself up, choose wisely, and when you do, trust that you have started this connection for a divine plan that is taking place.

Reflection

STOP: Evaluate those around you and what it will look like to have people you want around you. Find your supporters; let the love in.

LISTEN: Hear what is being said and let go of the story you have brought forward from the Program.

FEEL: As you receive the love, let the love land. Let it settle deep in your heart, and celebrate the steps you have made to be here.

9 LET GO AND LIVE IN YOUR HIGHEST EXPRESSION.

As you may recall in the beginning, we talked about Sally and her experience early on with the application. Sally was living from a place of being stuck. So much so that she had gone on from college, become an amazing marketing consultant, and left because she was building a family, only to end up feeling stuck in the place she loved.

Now, understand this: Sally was a great mom. Her kids loved her, and yet on the inside she was getting more numb with each passing day. Sally had been molested as a kid, from a family "friend." That is where so much got confused in Sally's head. As most kids were seeing Charlie Brown as a nice cartoon-character representation of childhood, Sally was relating to Charlie Brown, a real-life man, named Charlie Brown, the man who took advantage of an innocent kid, and that kid was Sally. Yes, oddly enough, his name was Charlie Brown.

This incident that took place created the Program that ran Sally's life. After each encounter with Charlie Brown, Sally would feel more distant from her parents. Where were they when she needed them? With her kids, she wanted to protect them in every way possible. She was and is an incredible friend because she loves everyone so much and cares so much to keep everyone safe. She loved me like I meant the world to her.

It was also a big curse for her, because when people would leave, Sally would cry and feel broken. There was a lot of crying that Sally could never truly explain. Sally's Program showed up in so many ways. This connection of "I am not safe and loved" played out everywhere Sally would turn. Her anger for Charlie Brown would secretly destroy her reality with her family. It was overwhelming for both Sally and her mom, as they would often fight. Sally would remember her mom as not caring, as she had spent much of Sally's childhood working to build a life for the family, as did her dad. Sally was also estranged from her dad, because he was not there to protect her and help her when she was most vulnerable.

When Sally first came to training, it was amazing how committed she was to getting all she could out of the training. This led to removal of the first layer of the echo program for Sally. She dove in, and during the first training she opened up. She allowed others in to see her; she was surrounded by love and support to allow her to feel safe and move forward. During the first training, I did not get to know her as well as I would in years to come; yet I knew she would someday let go and go deeper. See, for me at the time, we were in different vibrations. Later on, something opened up in her and we began to get closer.

Over the next couple of months, Sally's husband got a new job, and they had determined it was best for their family to move. The move was going to take them back north, where Sally was born, where the Program had been created, and the past would come to the surface. Sally closed off, not because of her desire not to support her husband. It was because she was in a supportive community and ready to connect—and here they were leaving.

Now was a chance to unpack the backpack or to close off. She chose to unpack and get clear. Sally is one of the strongest women I know, and has been one of my truest friends ever since she opened up. I am so blessed to have been part of this journey, because her birthing process has created a beautiful friendship in a place I was not even looking for it.

As we went into the second training, Sally was open. Immediately, she wanted to get clear and go a little deeper. She shared her fear of leaving and that she wanted the community and us with her. I remember the solution coming to the surface for Sally to take the community with her, and I would always be there when she called. It's a commitment I stand by in every way.

Give yourself space to dive in here and understand this. She gave it her all and opened up to how the Program was holding her back. She wanted to clear that she was in the struggle of what had happened in her childhood. She shared this in detail with her accountability buddy in training and continued until it was as clear as it could be at that time. She was able to allow herself to begin to let go of the story controlling her and her emotions. Although she had work to do for herself, she was ready to move forward.

This is what is next for you: get in and move forward. To reach your highest expression you must let go. This is similar to when you go out on Vision Quest, a Native American rite of passage, where a person is seeking to make a deeper connection with the Great Spirit or God. During that time, you give away something in order to make the deepest connection available with God.

Before I ever left to sit on the mountain, I detoxed everything in the last month before going out. Then for four days and three nights, I gave up shelter, food, and water to make a deeper conscious connection with God. That is where you are now in the process. It is time to give up something in order to make a great connection.

You know where you are now, and to reach your highest it is time to go beyond what you know. Your greatest part of you is connected to the source of all. So, to get there, you must understand your operating system is limiting because you are here in your body, within the earth's body. What can you give up to make the connection from your highest possible? Now is the perfect time to elevate your practice, your life, and your life practice.

Start with the practice of forgiveness and compassion, two of the greatest actions you can do here on earth.

> *Forgiveness is the action or the process of forgiving yourself or another and being forgiven.*

Here is a tool for you to use. Write out the following on a post-it, put it on the mirror, and do this two to three times a day as you brush your teeth:

I forgive you, ________, for ________.
I ask you, ________, to forgive me for ________.
Thank you for forgiving me.
I love you, ________. I love myself.
Thank you, ________, for loving me.
Thank you, God, for loving me.

There you go. Leave this up and continue to work with this until you can no longer fill in the blanks for ten straight days. The bonus is if something continues to surface, you can have an actual conversation. While asking for and giving forgiveness with an open heart, simply get on the phone or in person and state the above. No text messages—get connected, and get real. Get clear. Either way, the key is you allowing yourself to let go and move forward. Open up as forgiveness is for you. Forgiveness is for clearing the Program that ultimately has been holding you back.

Now let's look at the second action that will help to set you free: compassion.

Compassion is to have sympathy, genuine care and concern, for the suffering or misfortune of others.

Know that if you know there is a higher way of living and someone is doing less, they are doing so because they are either hurt, or they never were taught the higher road. You can move from a place of compassion and still protect yourself and stay out of harm's way. Clear to move forward to be free of fear. Make a choice for elevated living and keep going.

We all came from the same first cell which designed human nature. The first cell looked at itself and discarded what was not serving itself. Once it had removed what was not needed, it divided itself in half and gave of itself to make the next cell. That is what we are at the core of our being. We are here to give our best to another, and lift up the world.

One way to have compassion for someone else is to recognize what they have moved through. My grandma on my dad's side, Grandma Mary, would say, "We all have something, it's up to us to clear our something." Take care of all involved and move from the highest for all. Our human nature is to care for all. Put it into action. Remember, you are also someone, so as you forgive others, operating from the negative no longer serves you and is not living from your highest.

Now that you know, get into the action of forgiveness and compassion. Let go of your misses and perceived misses of others and lift up all. Hand over your guilt, shame, and hurt to the most high, forgive you, and have compassion for yourself. You are the greatest part of this equation.

Know this: for every trait you have, there is a positive and negative aspect of each one. There is a strength and weakness of each. Find the positive and strength in each. Find the positive characteristics and strengths in you, so that you can live in your highest. Learn to live in those aspects when it is truly appropriate. That is the access to your power.

Too much of anything is just too much. If you are stuck living in the zone of being nice, at some point you will be in the role of victim. If you are seeing "jerks" in your life, you are playing in the victim role somewhere. By living in balance, when it is appropriate, you may need to allow yourself to be cared for, and remember to get connected and centered. If you are always moving from a place of needing to be protected, you may show up in life as angry, bitter, or hateful, only because you want to live in the experience of being protected.

When you look at someone who you perceive to have the qualities of a jerk in any way, it is because of their desire to be cared for. Most of us know someone in life who comes across as arrogant, says mean things about others, or attacks when a perceived flaw is pointed out. Pause and recognize what is there. STOP, LISTEN, and FEEL what is real. Remember to eliminate the space of harm and move on with love, compassion, and forgiveness when needed.

Sally's story may seem heavy to some, yet we all have something, no matter how big or small. It just is, and clearing it is where the magic happens. Sally eventually moved and wanted to build the community where she lives now. She did not care how long it would take.

She just knew what she wanted. She gathered people who would be open to training, and she flew me in to train them. She began to watch it all unfold. As days passed, Sally watched everything open for others and knew that she could let more go. She again shared what had taken place in her life, in even greater detail than ever before. This time there was less emotion behind it and everything was clearing. The work she was doing was lifting her into a new vibration. At one point, she began to see how Charlie Brown was representing a tough life. The joke was that Lucy, or her mother, was representing the pressure the universe had created to help her see her greatest potential for forgiveness and compassion. Sally even saw how Snoopy could be just like the fun life she wanted for herself and her family. Once Sally had cleared and let another echo program go, we went to lunch to take a break. Sally was clear what was possible for her. I remember that all of a sudden, the sun came out and it was in the upper 60s, after snowing the day before. It is how it works. All of life is determined by your connection.

When we returned from lunch, we looked down at the door to the room we had rented for training and there it was, a Snoopy stuffed animal. For real, there it was: a Snoopy with his big grin. Sally looked at me and said, "How did you put this here?"

I said there was no way I would ever do that.

"Really?" she said. "Really?"

We went to all of the businesses in the same building and asked around. No one had left it. We checked with the students. No one had brought Snoopy. The Snoopy stuffed animal was there for Sally to see what was possible. It had meaning for us all to see what was there if we allowed it all in. Even as I type this, the thunder beings call out, in a completely beautiful, clear sky, here in Jacksonville, Florida. The thunder beings are calling loud and clear. It works like that. What we dial into is how the world shows up to and through us. Clean up your side of the street, and see how it all shows up around you.

It is the universe playing its song for us. Up, down, left, and right, forward and back. It is one song, and we are part of it. Uni-Verse. Think about it, one song. Understand how chaos actually creates one magical piece. At any point we can allow our lives to be different. What vibration are you orchestrating in the world?

People are all in their own Programs. We have a chance to move forward the way we want. Let go of the need to hold on to control.

There were days during our travels when I saw people were being malicious to us. It was interesting how people with hurt around their dads will reflect on some guy in their life. The same can be said for people with negativity from moments with their moms. Some people directly attacked and many others indirectly. Some people will spread dark energy by being vindictive and telling part truths to serve their needs.

I have witnessed people make statements that spew from the Program they are living. I recall when a woman once said to me, “Do you know karma? Karma is when a black man must come back and struggle with life, because in a former life, he was a plantation overseer and was cruel to slaves.”

I was fortunate. There I was in the practice beginning to see clearly where people are coming from and how connections were showing up in their life. As I moved through the Program, I had to reach out to my accountability buddies to begin to clear this deep root. At one point, she explained how her dad was undercover in the Klan, yet people she grew up with never believed he was undercover. I had been with many great teachers who taught karma, and this was not it. It is not this simple and may have nothing to do with struggling or not. So, I paused and moved ahead accordingly.

There was a need for me to practice compassion for myself and for this person; especially for myself, as I would only see from my hurt. The spreading of this darkness into the world was continuing to surface through me. My first action was to STOP, LISTEN with no response, and FEEL. I went to my accountability buddies and got their perspectives.

"Yes," they said, "Take care of you first."

Even my grandmother, one of my strongest coaches, laughed and said, "Time to get out, grandson, and leave all of that behind."

So, from that moment I had to go. With love in my heart, I began removing myself from the equation. It began to be about self-love. I am, as are you, part of this world, and it is time for us to clear and move forward.

Another person was spreading untruths around town about myself and Liz. I have a rule: if you gossip about anyone, you are gone, you can go, do your life, and remove me from the equation. I know that the reflections we see in life can be tough if we are not ready. So, with this person, who lives in an abusive relationship, I felt compassion for them, yet I will never play in their story.

Often when helping someone, they will turn their hurt to you in some way. It is up to you to pull away and let them be. Recognize that all reflection work is not yours to shift. The more you walk in this practice, the more you will begin to see the Program lose its power on you. Forgive and move forward with compassion, as not everyone knows what they are putting into the world.

Father, forgive them, for they do not know what they do

~LUKE 23:24

As Liz and I continued to move forward, we allowed ourselves to step away. Literally, we left town, and I began to dive into this book. Three weeks would pass, and after three days of writing I had the rough draft done. As we came back to pick up our belongings and move to Jacksonville, we headed to the beach to see what the waves looked like. As we neared the stop sign, just in front of us we saw what seemed to be these two ladies who caused us issues, crossing the street. These were two people that when we left for Atlanta had never met. So, who knows how that went down?

At first we saw Dee Dee cross the street, holding a child's hand. I paused and checked in, as this person was heavily limping. Then came the second woman, Cee Cee, holding her other daughter's hand. I smile as I write this, knowing Liz said, "It's time to keep moving." God has a huge sense of humor. No matter what, we wished them the best and kept moving. We rode in the car in silence, as we knew the universe was at play here and the two energies that had been in our lives were intertwined and being left behind. For some reason, they were now connected, and it was our time to ride off. We could choose to play in it or let it go. We chose to let it go and continue in the practice of self-love.

Later that evening, we went to the beach, and God began to provide us with more signs. We saw five guys on a father-and-son vacation weekend. They were fishing, and we all got to the beach at the same time. I am not a sport fisherman; I would rather feed my family if I feel a need to be a continuation in the circle of life. Yet as we walked up, they caught a four-foot bull shark. Then, when we came back, they caught a black-tip shark, again four feet long. They released them both, and that is when it landed for me as a sign. Keep moving, let them go, and that is what we did.

In the teachings of my elders, when something shows up in fours, it is time for a new beginning. Here we were with two sharks, each four feet long, and it was time for the two of us to embrace a new beginning. Watch the signs, as it is your time for a new beginning as well.

Be willing to move forward. We often remain tethered to where we once were. It is okay to have caught something and to release it. You do not always have to eat it. Clear your soul of anything holding on and move on up the road. Your feet are your soul's connection to your body and to the earth. They are the foundation where you touch the earth. You are moving around as your earth self. See the connection running in your operating system to all of your programs. If you need to evolve past any programs not serving your highest good, do so with ease in your heart.

Your highest expression is what you will know as your highest self in action. You can never miss the mark of what you are unaware of. Curious kids often wonder how rules work. I was a curious kid. Heck, I am still a curious kid about the rules of life, and I wanted to know the truth in the rules. Maybe many of you are like myself, you are just looking to see if the rule is worth keeping.

I recall as a kid being told that we would go to hell if we never accepted Jesus as our Lord and Savior. I never understood how my friend who was Jewish would go to hell because he did not know Jesus. I just couldn't get it, and no way could that be his fault. If Jesus had compassion, which he does—and God was a merciful God, which it is—and both are all knowing, which I was told they are, then how would they not know my friend was never taught about Jesus.

Sin is an immoral act considered to be transgressive against divine law.

What I saw were adults judging the life expression of another. How could one live a kind life, while another steals, harms others, and misses a mark that they choose to miss now to get a pass because at the last moment says, "I know Jesus as my Lord and Savior?" Does that get one a pass? Remember, God has a sense of humor.

I hear so many random people judge others for having many things, traditions, thoughts, and different expressions in life. There are many ways we make our way sacred and another person's way less sacred. The many ways that we judge another continues to build false Programs of separatism and creates big and small wars in the world. Who am I to judge my friend for being born into a Jewish family? We stayed friends for many years, as long as our journeys kept us together. To this day, I am sure he is just a good person. He went on to be a doctor to help others, while loving his family. So, I am sure we are headed in the same direction.

Judgement: drop it and find compassion, for when you judge, you have turned an eye onto yourself, to something deep within.

No need to turn a blind eye.

Stop judging, let's look a bit deeper. A boy born into pirating only knows pirating. They are often professional at stealing. He may even sell his siblings into sex trafficking. What will you do? Will you condemn him for being born into a life he doesn't know how to live differently, or will you help all the victims of a system missing the mark? You can help them see something else is possible. Will you build a new "jerk list," and another victim expression? Will you become the new oppressor?

What would your savior do with you?

Have compassion for others, for they know not what they do. Everyone wants to survive, to be protected, and FEEL love as well. What would you do if your only protection was to give your life up? Would you do it? If so, what are you waiting for? What are you willing to give your life for? No, not to go and take your life or take a life. Any coward can do that. Anyone can become a machine of destruction from the fears they live in. Can you become a life giver? Start with forgiveness and compassion.

Just because you know what you know, it never negates what someone else doesn't know. Be willing to preach sometimes with words. Be willing to be the example. Be it in action. Let's look at it in an easier way. A kid comes to play basketball, and he throws the ball in the wrong hoop. He is celebrating because he scored. Now we could celebrate with him because he scored his first basket; or we could yell and scream because he did the wrong thing in the game. What we could do is lift him up and teach him the game. We can hold anyone in their greatness; you just have to be willing to see beyond and raise them up. How will you choose to stand in the world and in the game of life?

My life has been full of games because my parents started me in sports at such an early age. My home in Maryland with my parents was great. My religious upbringing for me gave me a foundation to have a relationship with God, while also leaving me feeling guilty, hurt, and disconnected. I had to go and confess something to clear my soul. Funny thing was, I never felt guilty for my actions until I went to confession or had to face my dad. Not only did I confess to a guy I barely knew, I had to confess to my parents. So then comes the judgement. As time would pass, I would see what others did that could have been different. I would later have to put down my inner judge in life and move forward.

One day I went to jury duty. I was called for a trial of a young man who stole another kid's jacket. We were all asked questions to see if we could sit in on this case. Now, honestly, none of us were his peers; we were twice his age. Yet that is a whole other book. I could comply with all the questions. Then the judge asked if anyone felt they couldn't sit on the jury. I raised my hand.

She called me up and asked "Why do you feel you can't be on this jury?" I responded, "I have done enough in my life, a few things I would do differently, and I am not here to judge anyone. I have no desire to judge this young person and shape his life the way we have done to several kids today."

The response I received was quick, "Thank you for being the only person in my twenty years on the bench to say that, and to be willing to not judge another." Now I share this only to say it is time. We can stop judging and live differently. Is it right to swear on the Bible and judge another person? That seems to be living against the words in the Bible. How can one use the Bible as a life guide, and at the same time live from a system that judges others?

There seems to be a commitment to lie or live against the principles of what many say they follow; that is, 2.8 billion people practicing Christianity live from the judgements of right and wrong. I know there are actions, we call them sins, that don't fit a higher life, according to Jesus and the Bible. That does not create the right to judge others. The Bible is a guide to look at our own actions. Let's clear our own issues and Programs to inspire others and help all stand in a new way of the highest good. Now that you have that possibility to move from, will you open up to it? It starts with you. You want to have a new world? Then time to be it.

Be the change you want to see in the world.
~ Mahatma Gandhi

Let's allow Sally's story to be an example and activate the programs of forgiveness and compassion. Sally has gone on to forgive Charlie Brown. She moved forward to be free for herself, and so can you. What would your life be like if you could put down what has held you back? Sally has gone on to be the mom she knew she wanted to be. She let go of many fears that shaped her outlook for her kids. She shifted her relationship with her parents and husband. She went big and became a lighthouse for her community and opened a center to help all. This is what it can be like if you allow yourself to release the connection that is holding you back.

Let's build a new home to move from through life. Get solid and be willing to stand firm.

Those who stand for nothing fall for anything.
When you stand for nothing, you fall for everything.
~ Alexander Hamilton

See how standing in your power fits; try it on. Move around in the new vibration. See if it is getting you to your new destination, the street called desire.

10 SHARE THIS WITH THE WORLD.

Jesus was not Christian. Buddha was not Buddhist. What I wish to be is the best Sid I can be, to be an example that others may see and choose to be if it is best for them. It is truly a blessing to see the players I have coached go on to assist another in their greatness. To see people who have seen me as a parent go on to raise their kids in a similar fashion, go on to be great. To see those who call me teacher, go on to help someone else be the best student they can be. As it was said before:

Give a man a fish, and you have fed him once.
Teach him how to fish and you have fed him for a lifetime.
~ Chinese Proverb

The only way you can share this is to live the practice of forgiveness and compassion.

As I said earlier, we spent a year in our car with 31,000-plus miles and many flights. We stayed at friends' houses. We stayed in hotels. We slept in our car and kept going until we found our place. Our desert in this life was the road. We were put on the road to reflect and see what was coming so we could lift the world to a higher place, wherever we were. We were blessed, as every day was easy because we had each other.

What we knew is I felt like I was going to die if I did not leave Baltimore and hit the road. Trapped in my own skin and loved by Liz, we went to build our new life together. We were living it, being us. "Peace Across America," peace through the world. We moved in our way and have gotten to know each other on another level. I had to clean up my stuff that had gotten in my way of my highest expression. Then came the pandemic. For me it was time to go further in. To go into my faith, to face and transform my relationship with racism, to stand for me, and my relationship with the most high.

Before we went to the Dominican Republic, we were about to rent a house. Several people came to the medicine circle I was leading in Santa Rosa Beach, Florida. The medicine circle, or healing circle as many have called it, is where I lead energy transmissions to allow the Great Spirit or God to come through and raise the vibration for all involved. This is where I first met Dee Dee. She came to heal her connection to her past, something she described as her past lives in Egypt. It was an interesting start, as many things were said to allude to her connection to those around her, even calling me her brother. It was a great night, where many had moved forward and opened up to many shifts for themselves.

I had to teach class the next day, and Dee Dee was coming in to get a massage. Liz and I were looking for a house to live in, so I left a note on Dee Dee's car to see if she knew of anyone renting their house. It just so happened that she was looking for people to house sit; as she said, her house would be protected by light by having light workers live there. This seemed really easy, until we moved in. First came the first night asking us to sit with her as she led a prayer night; it was not our way of praying, and we remained open. Then came the question, "Will you pay the electric bill?" Sure. Then other things came to be, all of which seemed easy. She left for the islands, and we left for the Dominican Republic. When we came back, we were stuck where we were. The pandemic of 2020 had started. She was in her house in Alabama, and we were stuck in her house in Freeport, Florida.

A lesson of old for me is simple; honor your word as in the end that is all you have. We were asked to pay the heat bill, so we did, and hold the energetic light in the house. We had said yes, and it made it easy for us to have a roof over our head and to avoid being locked in to a rental for a year, when maybe we might want to do something else. Now, understand with the pandemic hitting, our stay was longer than any of us had expected. Yet we made it through with gratitude for all that God had provided, us as we moved forward.

It is all a journey, and you will have a series of tests to see and move through until the work is done. Over time, living in Dee Dee's house became a burden, more than it was worth. More and more continued to pile up. Liz and I worked every day through the pandemic, looking for ways to keep our center open. We created so many things to keep us going. Dee Dee's way of being made sure I was able to see the situation, while masking it all by giving a "helping hand." It was a double entendre, definitely open to interpretation. I knew I had a mission to spread this word with the world. I was searching to see if anyone would be able to connect, and a show was created on YouTube, "The Great Work." We worked and worked to pull off the work to touch others. I learned a lot from each person involved, while continuing to see how to grow my mission. There are times it may get difficult to hold your balance inside. As one healer said, this is about you, you becoming you fully, and continuing to move forward.

You name it, everywhere we turned, we were living from a place of trust in God. Dee

Dee helped us see just how we could hold our space in the world. At one point, she even made sure we got to see whether we needed to keep her gun with us or not, as we slept in the house. Dee Dee made sure we had the view from many angles. Were we going to fall back to a Program of fear or move into the Program we wanted to live from? Lessons came forward and propelled us to leave Santa Rosa Beach and find our new home.

As soon as we got out, many things began to clear up. We left for Atlanta and had time to center ourselves before we would journey back to Florida, and move to Jacksonville. It was interesting how, when we moved beyond this connection to the darkness, we found the light opened up to show us the way.

Liz found a job; studios we connected to invited us to join their communities. In a week, we found a house we loved, and we moved forward. This was the key. We had to trust us, and move forward together.

It became apparent that we were the keys to spreading the message, as are you. We are the ones to be the examples for others to live from if they choose. I've seen it time and time again. When I hold the Program of love or peace, others align to it. So here it is, time for you to be the lighthouse for others as well.

The experience on the road landed seven incredible lessons to share with others:

1. **Know thy self and to thy own self be true. ~ William Shakespeare, Hamlet**
   As I talk about it in *Yoga and Life Empowerment*, the truth will set you free. So often I have seen people get caught in their truth, not 'the truth." Often their truth looks like an opinion of what happened or what they think happened. Sometimes it is the story they have from another. Often just seeking the truth of what took place will set you free. The actual truth of the moment is: something happened. He threw a ball. She killed a bug. My mom said this or that. When we put descriptions on the facts, our interpretations on it are often where we get lost in the echo of the Program. He threw the ball high. What is high to one is low to another. She is so mean cause she killed a bug. Some see it as part of propelling the bug forward into evolution. My mom is nice when she says this, and is a jerk when she says that. You can see how the descriptions give way to adding or subtracting in some way from the truth. When you add the descriptions, you have already become the judge, when the truth is:

something happened. Not good or bad, not right or wrong; it just is.

Know you. Clear the Program and be true to you so you can be free to find your highest.

2. **Know your team**
   Know your team and keep your circle tight. Like attracts like. So, who are the people you are around the most? It is said if you want to know a person, know the top five people they are around, and you will know what they are like. When it comes to keeping your circle tight, it is one way to know who you are. It is also important to keep your circle tight in order to know that you are supported and that you have a sounding board you can trust, one that will hold you in your highest good. Everyone can use a little help now and then. Know who you put on your team. Stay connected with your team and know who will support you every day.

3. **Have compassion**
   Have compassion for all you meet. You never know what anyone has been through in life. What we know is, even if we have experienced the exact same thing on the exact same

day at the exact same time, our view is a unique view. So, we are sitting in different views. By sitting with compassion, we allow space for love to come forward. By sitting with compassion for another, we allow love to come forward for ourselves, as well.

4. **Get centered**
   Get centered in what you want; live from there as you live for the highest of all. We found it, and made Jacksonville our home. Your dream is out there for you as well. There is a song I picked up along the way, "Sunday Best," by Surface. Check it out sometime; you just have to shift the vibration. The Universe is Uni-Verse; it is one song, and you are an instrument in a vibration of beautiful music.

5. **Know "the Program"**
   Take your time and listen. The Program is running in the background. There are many Programs. No judgements; they are just Programs and can be shifted, as needed. Go deeper when you see a Program not serving you. Identify it and move forward. Practice SLF (STOP, LISTEN, FEEL)

often to bring forward the three **C**s: **C**lear, **C**onnect, and **C**enter. This is your chance to move into the life of your dreams. No-thing to fear. You are exactly where you need to be.

6. **Feel and Know**
   As you use STOP, LISTEN, and FEEL, you will become less reactive. Listen to your feelings at a deeper level to hear the truth as your guide. Let go of the idea that your feelings are good or bad, right or wrong, and just focus on what they are guiding you to. Allow the positive and/or negative feelings to guide you to where you want to go. All feelings are there as God's communication to point you to your destiny. As a baby, we learn this almost instantly, with feelings we like and dislike. Be willing to get to the feeling, observe, and move forward accordingly. Initially, it may take some time to know that in time you will flow through to the next place with ease.

7. **Keep going**
   You are here to live life. Keep going. Move consciously in the direction of what you desire and know all is taken care of. Where you are now is your

destiny. Do the best you can where you are, and allow it to move you forward with ease. Keep going.

Follow your bliss and the universe will open doors where there were only walls.
~ Joseph Campbell

Let your life be the greatest message you can give to another person. Preach all the time by allowing your life to be the message all can see. This will be the greatest impact we all can have; just keep going.

11 BE WILLING TO START AGAIN.

We have begun anew, and the feeling is rebirth. We set out to find our home, our community to live in, and a place to lay our roots. We are here now, and it is our time to live the life of our dreams.

Our last step came when we were choosing where to live. Understand, we were in the midst of living in Santa Rosa Beach, Florida, where we had landed during the pandemic of 2020. Life had been at a standstill for everyone around the world, and now it was time for us to see what was next. We started to recognize our time of living in Santa Rosa Beach was coming to an end. We were set to move out on July 1st, and had told Dee Dee we could leave early, if needed. I was getting closer to hearing the voice of guidance all the time.

I could hear when things just did not fit and feel when I was in alignment. Liz and I began to look deeper into just what it would look like for us to live the life of our dreams. After traveling 31,000 miles, we had connected to three places: Rosemary Beach or Jacksonville Beach in Florida, and San Diego, California. All of these had been places that had grown dear to us in many ways. Rosemary Beach was where we were married and will always be a great memory for us. Several people had been kind to us on our travels. Jacksonville Beach was a place we stopped many times in our travels. We resonated with so many people, and it often seemed like a place we felt at ease. Then there was San Diego and the charm we connected with as we went to start our honeymoon.

This was the time to allow the guidance to show through and make sure we landed where we would feel at home and flourish in every way.

There were things that would come into our unconscious minds. We would have to see with clarity in order to move forward. In an unconscious state, we typically move from a place of fear and can often be in reaction mode. When we were in Santa Rosa Beach, we had negative moments and people that came into our reality. The more those moments would come, the more we became guarded to protect ourselves from the darkness ahead. Black Lives Matter was a big movement that shed light on how we did not fit where we were. We know that diversity is important to us.

I got a phone call one Monday that said we were going to need to make sure we were moved out by Friday, which happened to be my birthday. It was interesting how things were playing out. I was told I had a lack of gratitude. I was told as long as I was staying in her house, Dee Dee was entitled to tell me her opinion on how to live my life. Then, as soon as Liz would get on the phone with her, the story would change. We began to see that Dee Dee was treating me differently than Liz. There was an undercurrent of racism or male hate that seemed to surface.

Some things I sit with, and this was one I had to clear ASAP.

We left the house and went over to an appointment where Liz had to lead a Life Empowerment Coaching session. When we got there, we were greeted by a friend, Carmen, the mother of Liz's coaching client. Carmen is a tremendously caring person. As we sat in the living room, Carmen asked, "How are you?"

Now this was all fresh, so I said, "Well, we were just told we need to be out of the house we are staying in, by Friday."

"Wait," Carmen said, "It is Monday. You mean *this* Friday, during the celebration of your birthday?"

"Yes, this Friday," I responded. Carmen replied, "Well, we just bought this house, and we are leaving for Europe, so we could have you stay here. You are my friends, and I would rather do that than rent it out. That is what friends do."

In the Native American tradition, we take on relatives when it is appropriate. One of the biggest relationships you can take on is that of a friend; because if you are a friend, you are willing to give up anything in the name of friendship. So, yes, Carmen is a friend for sure, as she took care of us, and we are forever grateful for her.

Carmen's grace began a process that allowed us to move forward with great ease. When we got back, I contacted Dee Dee to let her know we would be out tomorrow. It was interesting. In one moment, we were told to leave. Then we say we are out, and we are told, "No, I need you to stay to make sure my house is okay." What we began to realize, more like confirm, was it was time to move forward.

"The hits just keep on coming." This was the shift in the journey that would continue to test our resolve. Would we finish or would we quit? We were determined to keep going.

At some point, Carmen realized that she had a major potential income being lost on her home as a rental property for the summer. Carmen then asked if we would mind moving.

Lending us this particular home could be a setback for her family. Yet Carmen was also willing to let us stay, if we thought we needed to. Truly a selfless act. In the high season, she stood to make as much as ten thousand dollars a week. It was an easy thought; how could we say no?

We had some friends who had invited us to stay at their home, and then that fell through. Carmen welcomed us to her home in Atlanta, where this book would unfold and our journey would begin to come to an end.

We had evaluated everything and were ready to make a choice to move to Jacksonville. In our hearts, we just knew. As soon as we made that choice, doors began to fly open. Liz got interviews to be a counselor, and I got calls from coaches asking me to work with their teams, as a coach that would later be known as the "secret weapon." We connected to yoga studios and opened up to all that was coming forward. When clarity came, I knew I was ready to write, and in three days I had the first draft of this book complete.

It is amazing that when it is time, everything is just a heartbeat away. We knew that, after working every day through the pandemic, and staying focused on what we wanted, everything would happen in God's time, and it would flood in.

We had arrived at a new place. We had taken the horse by the reins and were ready to ride.

The subconscious mind is running various programs all the time. It is running a program we may not see, and the way to see them is by what continues to show up in your life. At this point, we were seeing things clearly and it was our time to guide the Program to what we wanted. Remove the old and begin anew.

So much was coming through with divine timing, and all would fall into place in a grand way. It was time for us to apply the practice of STOP, LISTEN, and FEEL to make a choice and connect with what would fulfill our lives and our hearts' dreams. The conscious mind has the ability to override all other thoughts. You must first know what you want and guide your thoughts accordingly. By staying disciplined, you can bring it all forward.

Once we knew where we were going to go, it was up to us to see it through. While in Atlanta, we had a chance to see friends, complete work, head to the waterfalls, and keep going. We took a day trip to Jacksonville and planned to find our house on a Monday, a week before Liz was to start her job. We looked all over the internet and found a couple of places, so we figured we would pick from what we saw. We had some extra time, and planned that Liz could stop by her new job. Oh yeah, I forgot: she got the job. Of course she did. She is amazing.

When we left, I said to Liz, "Okay, here it is. We go to Jacksonville, and we can move forward in the flow of the moment, and all will be great." Our parents were excited to know we were going. All ducks in a row.

Everything seemed great. We were on our way. Now, mind you, I recruited all over the country and was rarely ever in traffic. It was one of the things I would work on as an early manifestation practice, before I knew about the Program. So, when we hit traffic, we were surprised. When we started, I had said to Liz, "Okay, let's stay present to what we allow in, as we can work this day and complete the task."

Well, we were forty minutes out, and what happened? Liz received a text message from someone who had often been a negative in moments. I thought, "Oh no, is she sending salt into the game?" This was actually my old Program and had nothing to do with her.

Right then, a cop appeared in front of us, directing everyone off the highway. Mind you, I was just grateful I was not a little earlier and part of the accident. We got off, and forty minutes turned into three hours. We finally got into Jacksonville, and Liz canceled going to see her new job, and we needed a place to live. It turned out, when we saw the house, it was nowhere near what we wanted. It was dark, and the cost was going to chew up our budget. At that point, we had to recalibrate and get back on track. Start again!

We looked around at different neighborhoods. We came to a community where there happened to be a lady sitting outside. I said, "Hold on, let's ask her what she thinks."

"Hi, what do you think of living here?" I said to her.

She responded, "Well, it is nice, but I own a couple of condos at Villas on the Marsh. That is where I say you should live, but none of mine are open or for sale."

We drove over anyway, and the gates were closed. I remember saying to Liz, "Well, at least it is a gated community. That would be good." We got in the car and went to the beach. I said, "We want to live at the beach, so let's go."

That was all we needed. The ocean is one place where we can **C**enter, and then go forward. We settled back into the space we hold for one another. I mean, we traveled 31,000 miles in ease; we could allow this to be easy. We grabbed something to eat and headed back. I remember watching my own Programs play out. I was able to see a way clear. I was able to see how my program of worry about wasting money came up. Nothing to do but just STOP feeding it.

So, there we were, back in Atlanta, with four days until we planned to move to Jacksonville. We had some great things come forward, and one was meeting Idris, a realtor who was going to help us find a place to rent. We figured this would be easiest in the short-term. He said he liked us, so he was going to send us properties that fit what we wanted. His company is called Red Zone Properties, so I knew we were back in the flow. Who has a real estate company about football? There are always signs; we just have to be willing to look for them.

We narrowed our search down, flowed through a few speed bumps, and moved into the Villas of the Marsh on Saturday. Idris and the lady we met when we visited Jacksonville were not acquainted, and yet both got us to the Villas of the Marsh—another sign. A day late, yet right on time. Have faith and keep going. It will always work out for your highest good if you let it. We are living proof, as are so many others. You just have to have faith and keep going.

You are here, check in. Periodically I will STOP, LISTEN, and FEEL. I sit and check in. Is there anything I need to get clear on? Is there anything holding me back from my greatest potential? There is a magic question I sit with: "Are you happy?" It may take time, yet being happy is just a heartbeat away. I have seen that in a single heartbeat, the world can shift around you. It is my faith in that realization that reminds me it is all a heartbeat away.

Are you at peace? Happiness and peace are an inside job, and only you know if you have it. It is the middle, the zero point from where all is birthed. The zero point where all is possible. The zero point where all negative points have been cleared up. The zero point where all positive points grow from. At any time if you realize you are off point, off line, off the flow for the greatest possible in your life, utilize your tool of SLF to get back to zero or nothing and start again.

You now have this book and can get to the other side of anything at any point. Let go. If you need anything, find me. Here is my website: www.SidMcNairy.com. Contact me anytime. Even a coach sometimes needs a coach. The moment you realize you are off track, come back, and start over and go forward.

Let he that would move the world first move himself.
~ Socrates

As you continue through this journey, stay present. As my grandmother says, "Even God leaves when you aren't present." Let that sink in as you prepare for the next step on this path. Open up to what you are present to in every moment going forward, more to come.

May the light shine through you always.

All of life is determined by your connection.

I love you, so let me leave you with one last nugget. Those who know me know I refrain from telling jokes. You may ask why. It is another simple place for me to connect. When one tells a joke, there are a lot of things that come forward from them. One is that someone is offended. Someone may not understand and think I am saying the truth.

Finally, I know the power of the connection I have established with the creator of all. Because God is on my team, my words create my reality, jokes or not.

You make plans, and they say God is laughing. From my view, that is the ultimate joke. God knows that until you consciously know what you are creating in the world, there is more work to be done. We are all in this together, let's finish and allow everyone to live the life of their dreams.

All of life is determined by
your connection.

When you find yourself in a moment when something is off, when you know you don't want something, start over and read this book again!

The End . . . The Beginning

CPSIA information can be obtained
at www.ICGtesting.com
Printed in the USA
LVHW052228031220
673096LV00044B/692/J

9 780997 538397